OXFORD MONOGRAPHS ON
SOCIAL ANTHROPOLOGY

General Editors

E. E. EVANS-PRITCHARD   J. G. PERISTIANY

T. K. PENNIMAN   I. SCHAPERA

Oxford University Press, Amen House, London E.C.4

GLASGOW NEW YORK TORONTO MELBOURNE WELLINGTON
BOMBAY CALCUTTA MADRAS KARACHI LAHORE DACCA
CAPE TOWN SALISBURY NAIROBI IBADAN ACCRA
KUALA LUMPUR HONG KONG

Möjut Awol—Head of Dakotiaŋ lineage of Dari clan

Chiefs and Strangers

A STUDY OF
POLITICAL ASSIMILATION
AMONG THE MANDARI

BY

J. C. BUXTON

OXFORD
AT THE CLARENDON PRESS
1963

© *Oxford University Press 1963*

PRINTED IN GREAT BRITAIN
AT THE UNIVERSITY PRESS, OXFORD
BY VIVIAN RIDLER
PRINTER TO THE UNIVERSITY

TO
THE MANDARI
AND IN PARTICULAR THE
PEOPLE OF DARI

PREFACE

THE material presented here was collected during eighteen months spent among the Mandari of the southern Sudan between 1950 and 1952, and a short visit of a month in 1958. Between these periods the Anglo-Egyptian Condominium became the Republic of the Sudan.

Initially I was asked by the Sudan government to study the Mandari because they were considered to present certain administrative problems. One example of this was the uneasy and sometimes violent relations between the Mandari and their neighbours, the Aliab Dinka; another was the failure of the traditional Mandari chiefdoms (re-grouped into larger divisions by the administration) to co-operate with one another, or even be on good terms.

The geographical isolation of the Mandari (particularly that of the western peoples described in detail in this account) and the consequent lack of knowledge about them had given the impression to administrators and others that they were not co-operative, as well as being obviously less sophisticated than better-known and more frequently visited neighbours.

Mandari country is certainly hard to work in. It is the more isolated for being situated on the borders of Equatoria Province, with headquarters at Juba, and adjacent to Bahr el Ghazel, administered from Wau. It lies at the farthest point from both headquarters: a dead-end leading nowhere. At the time of my arrival roads and communications were bad, and in addition the continual movement of a large part of the Mandari population over their country into Aliab Dinka grazing-lands made consistent investigation difficult. In the rains there was the problem of my own movement, and of retaining any regular contact with the outside world.

Some of these conditions had changed when I returned in 1958. External and internal communications had improved, and there was the possibility of relatively quick and regular contact. A government elementary school had been opened at Tali, and a small Catholic mission under two European Verona Fathers established some miles away. There was a noticeably greater sophistication of outlook among the Mandari, and a succession of

British and Sudanese administrators had made repeated and re-
warding contacts with them.

I also spent four months on the Nile with other peoples called
'Mandari'. I found these to be largely composed of non-Mandari
stocks, and I do not include the results of that visit here.

In this account I deal with Mandari political structure, with
relations between political groups, and with events which the
Mandari see as part of their history and which relate directly to
many current political situations. A characteristic of Mandari
society has always been political assimilation of different kinds
—that of dependent strangers to established patrons, that of new
groups to older ones, that of the politically weak to the politically
powerful. The ability to assimilate individuals and small groups
of people into the society and imbue them with strong feelings
for the Mandari culture and way of life may, in fact, have been one
of the reasons why the Mandari have succeeded in retaining their
independence in the face of southward pressure by their powerful
Dinka neighbours.

The same flexibility has not been shown by the Mandari in relation to certain changes inaugurated by the administration during
the beginning of this century. Thus, some of the new administrative divisions made up of small chiefdoms have failed to become
real corporate units. This is partly due, I believe, to the kind of
units early administrators were forced to amalgamate in order to
carry out effective administration, and to the sparsity of information
about them, which sometimes resulted in hostile combinations.
Many underlying tensions are explained by the fact that while the
Mandari have a uniform culture and social organization, they
have always lacked any wide-scale political solidarity of the kind
which has now been imposed from without. It would appear that
fragmentation was the essence of the political system, a single-
village chiefdom being the largest unit with full political functions.
The chiefdom has always had strong individualistic and partisan
interests, which were only inhibited by varying kinds of self-
interest.

Because of the interrelated factors of history and social structure,
it has been necessary to present this account on two levels—as
a study of the development of contemporary Mandari political
groups through what the people themselves can say of their

history, and as a sociological analysis of a functioning political system. Two methods of investigation were used. To obtain historical data, I visited about thirty village chiefdoms which claimed that they had been politically independent before the government amalgamations. Most of what the Mandari know of their past is contained in stories of movements of groups of people under important ancestors of ruling descent lines, and during my visits to different parts of the country my time was spent in collecting these histories and their supporting genealogies. The small scale of the country made the collection of these data possible. Mandari history shows a distinct process of spread and extended domination by certain groups holding powerful chiefdoms, with a decline, or even a political extinction, of others, which is sometimes directly linked with the rise of a rival neighbour. The implications of this rise and fall are very clear today, and I have included material to substantiate it because it is essential to an understanding of how the past affects present political situations.

I also made an intensive study of a single chiefdom, living for nine months in the central village of one of the larger ones, and making short visits to other chiefdoms with whom social, political, and economic relations were regular and important.

Any contemporary study of African political institutions is complicated by the presence of external administrations, and it may even be argued that to attempt to present indigenous institutions as they were is now unrealistic. However, in the case of the Mandari, I feel this attempt is justified, mainly because it is still possible to get a fairly clear picture of the old Mandari chiefdoms, and even to observe directly the workings of many indigenous political institutions. In the southern Sudan administration came later than in many parts of Africa, and inaccessibility and the difficult conditions of the interior made its work of re-organization slower. Not only are there individuals alive who remember the beginnings of the new system, but the traditional political divisions are still important.

Throughout this account I shall try to make it clear when I am describing institutions which are directly observable and functioning, as opposed to those which have been described to me by people who profess to have experienced them or to remember them from hearsay.   J. C. B.

ACKNOWLEDGEMENTS

I STUDIED the Mandari at the request of the government of the Anglo-Egyptian Sudan which generously paid my air passages to and from the Sudan and much of my transport about the country. I would like to thank all those in the government and the administration who showed me so much kindness and hospitality. It would be impossible to mention them all by name, but I would particularly like to thank Mr. and Mrs. Dingwall, Colonel and Mrs. Molloy, and Mr. and Mrs. Peter Tripp; also Sayed Abdul Rahim Said for his help when he was District Commissioner Mandari, Sayed Mahmoud Abu Sinena, and Mr. John Hannah. Mr. J. F. Tierney, Mr. B. A. Lewis, and Mr. Charles de Bunsen were in Juba at different times during my stay and gave me much encouragement. I also thank the Sudanese officials who arranged my return visit in 1958 and gave me support on the spot, particularly Sayed Macawi Suleiman Akrat and Sayed Clement Mboro. The C.M.S. Missionaries kindly put me up in Juba on this occasion.

My Mandari friends are without number and to them all I owe a great debt for their patience and kindness. My eighteen months in their country were very happy ones. I would particularly mention the Chief and people of Dari, in whose village I lived for nine months, and members of other chiefdoms with whom I spent shorter periods.

Consistent encouragement and help were given me by Makelele Nyayo of Mandari, now a Police Officer, and I am grateful to him for allowing me to use those Mandari clan histories which he had collected. I would also record the help of Pudö Diyö.

At the Institute of Social Anthropology, Oxford, I owe a great debt to my supervisor Dr. R. G. Lienhardt on whose help and ideas I have drawn throughout my anthropological work. When I arrived in the Sudan he was working with the Dinka, and came to meet me and then spent a few weeks with me in Mandari country. I am also deeply indebted to Professor Evans-Pritchard for his interest and the inspiration of his writings. Dr. J. Beattie and Dr. Peristiany made useful criticisms of my draft.

I thank my cousin, Mr. P. P. Howell, O.B.E., for introducing me to Anthropology in the first place and for hospitality in the Aliab and Malakal.

The draft of this book was read at various stages by Mrs. Marian Carr, Miss P. Gurney, and Miss M. Leon. Professor Evans-Pritchard and Dr. Lienhardt kindly read the proofs.

Some of the material on clientship has already been published in *Sudan Notes and Records*, vol. xxxviii, 1957.

CONTENTS

LIST OF PLATES

MAPS

FIGURES

INTRODUCTION

I

THE PEOPLES CALLED 'MANDARI'

IN the widest sense the name 'Mandari' refers to pastoralists who occupy two separate and distinct lands. One of these is a Nile water-frontage of about fifty miles on both river banks, the other is a sprawling country inland to the west.[1] Both of these Mandari speak dialects of Bari, and like the Bari, have ultimately been classified through language with the Nilo-Hamitic-speaking peoples.[2] This is not, however, a very satisfactory classification—partly because the Mandari language in fact differs considerably from Bari (the Nilo-Hamitic language with which it has the closest affinities), and also because in other ways the Mandari have so little in common with the larger Nilo-Hamites such as the Kipsigis, Masai, or Nandi that a linking with them on a purely linguistic level seems unrealistic. Even the Bari, of whom the Mandari are claimed to be (and would probably agree to being) an offshoot, do not appear from the available literature to be typically 'Nilo-Hamitic'. There is no doubt, however, that a Nilo-Hamitic element has formed part of the evolutionary process of the Mandari, but other influences would seem to have been at least as important, if not more so. Mandari country was certainly subjected to the impact of migrating peoples, including probably the Luo, and in Mandari, Nilotic features showing affinity with Luo-speaking peoples such as the Acholi and Lango are apparent. Further, in recent times, a known and direct linguistic and cultural borrowing from Aliab

[1] The total Mandari territories lie roughly between 32° East and 30° 30′ West and 6° 15′ North and 5° 20′ South, in Equatoria Province of the Sudan Republic. (See map on p. 2.)

[2] Tucker and Bryan, *Non-Bantu Languages*, International African Institute, Oxford, 1956, pp. 106–17 and 149–56.

Dinka and Atuot neighbours, which still continues, has added new Nilotic elements. The location of the Mandari between the sizeable Nilote and Nilo-Hamitic blocks to their north and south has made their country subject to influences from both sides.

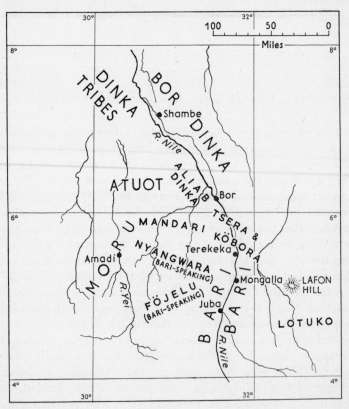

MAP I.

Apart from the difficulty of general classification, there is doubt in my mind whether the two separated Mandari peoples should be considered together. For instance, the use of the name 'Mandari' for the Nile-dwellers is open to question. Both regions are now, however, regarded as a single administrative area, and a vague sense of being one people is admitted by both, and extended to other Bari-speakers, on account of cultural and linguistic affiliations which distinguish all more sharply from the Dinka to the north.

Paradoxically, however, the inland, western Mandari have regular interrelations with Aliab Dinka and Atuot, and only intermittent ones in certain places with river-dwelling Mandari.

The positions of all Mandari peoples is shown on the map at the end of the book. They are as follows:

The Western Inland Mandari

About fifteen thousand people who speak of themselves as being the true Mandari live in the western inland country. They form a buffer between the large pastoral Atuot and Aliab Dinka and the masses of the agricultural Moru. In the south-east they are flanked by Bari-speaking Nyangwara, with whom they have had consistently friendly relations. On the eastern side their land is separated from that of the river-dwelling Mandari by a broad, arid plain, largely uninhabited and in some parts about seventy miles across.

Mandari-land is sparsely inhabited by scattered groups, from Kor, on the Atuot boundary, to the south-western Moru village of Madi Biti. In the east Mount Tindalu marks the end of permanent settlement, but grazing extends to Khor Gwir, a waterway which enters the Nile in the Aliab swamps. The northern part of the uninhabited plain is also repeatedly crossed by Mandari cattle migrating to Dinka dry-season grasslands.

All the people in this country are spoken of as 'Mandari Gworoŋa' by the Nile-dwelling Mandari, from the small clan 'Gworoŋa', on the eastern Mandari boundary.

Nile-dwelling 'Mandari'

I also give a few details about the river-dwelling peoples generally called 'Mandari' and lumped together without qualification with their inland neighbours.

River-dwelling 'Mandari' live south of the Aliab and Bor Dinka, on the west and east banks of the Nile, along a narrow strip of country behind the flood-line. They number about 20,000.

Early intermingling of populations makes it difficult to place them conclusively. The valley's large expanses of seasonally-flooded island grazing, attracted wanderers searching for new home-lands and migrants from surrounding tribes who intermarried with earlier established peoples. Constant fighting and struggles for domination of the river banks are recalled by all living here. Clan histories and genealogies I collected give the following levels of population.

i. *The Tsera*

The Tsera claim to have been very early established. They straddle both Nile banks and are certainly the people described as Shir, Shyr, or Tshièrr by nineteenth-century writers. Although remembering no single founder, they claim to be one people, who formerly spoke a Tsera language, now replaced by a Bari dialect. The Tsera say that the small size of their political units and the lack of cohesion among them is due to frequent movement up and down and across the Nile.[1]

ii. *Böri (known as Köbora on the west bank)*

The east bank Böri and west bank Köbora are the most numerous Nile people, and now hold two administrative chiefships.

Lafon Hill, a small mountain about sixty miles east of the Nile and a dispersal point for a series of migrations, is central in their history. At Lafon I was given accounts of early Böri movements.

The first inhabitants of the hill were in fact of Shilluk-speaking stock, whose descendants say they still understand the Shilluk language. They are the Pugari rain-making clan who 'own' the hill, and who told me how originally two brothers, Nykaja and Juro, found it and settled there, one at the top and the other at the bottom.

The Böri (also called Pöri and Phaari) came later, and were of Anuak stock. They are now known as 'Lokora', or 'Böri Lokora', a name given to them by neighbouring Acholi. The Böri broke off from a Luo migration the rest of which went eastwards to Anuak land. The place where they separated from their Anuak-founding kin was Pöri, a country near the Kit river (called Borgilo by the

---

[1] Tsera live as follows:

West Bank.

    At Tombek, and north and south of this village.
    At a small lagoon north of Moni lagoon.
    Around Terekeka.

East Bank.

    In and around Bukö.
    In well-defined villages from Yöbisok on the Bor Dinka boundary to a few
    miles north of Gameiza.

Böri) in present-day Bari territory. The Böri people now call Pöri, 'Wi-pöri', meaning 'Pöri—a place left behind'. An ancestress, Aboŋa, came to Lafon when her husband died at Adoŋo in Pöri and the rest of his people moved to Anuak. She brought her infant son, Leballa, with her and settled with Dimo, an important ancestor of the Shilluk Pugari. History describes her as an astute woman, who by cleverly manipulating a case over the blinding of her son in one eye, gained, as compensation, the overlordship of Lafon Hill. On her death her son succeeded as chief, while the Pugari clan retained the ownership of the mountain itself and rain-power. Aboŋo's descendants are the Yatwö clan who hold the Lafon chiefship:

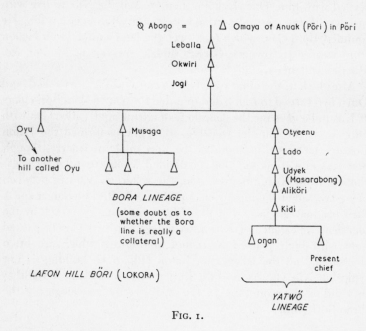

Fig. 1.

Accounts of the way in which part of the Böri left Lafon for the Nile vary according as they are given by the people now at Lafon or by those in the Nile village of Kösumba. Lafon accounts say that the separation took place in Wi-pöri after a fight, and that the ancestor of this particular group went straight to Kösumba and never reached Lafon. At Kösumba, however, Böri elders spoke of their founders as three of four brothers who lived at Nuggi, a mountain in Liria. The fourth stayed there, founding the Lokoya (related to the Böri, according to all groups). The other three left when the fourth brother, who was a rain-maker, loosed his cows and found water and grass while the others found only scorched earth: they accused him of withholding the rain. A quarrel also followed over a bead swallowed by his infant daughter, which led to the child being dissected. The three brothers, by-passing Lafon, or only stopping for a short while there, settled near Kösumba. The bull of one brother is then said to have heard cows lowing and to have gone off unobserved to a lagoon to graze. When it was eventually found, the brothers met the owner of the cows, 'a Mandari, named Nyumbour, with four eyes, two in his head and two on his shoulders'. They settled with him. One, Lukölö, then crossed the Nile to live with in-laws, having married a girl of Gwele, a small indigenous line. He founded Ilörö clan, which took over the land round Moni lagoon from weak early owners, Gwele, Budak, Nyarkiteŋ, Modoŋ, &c. His descendants are the Köbora.

After he left, the other two, Könye and Duru'le, quarrelled, and Duru'le returned to Lafon and founded the Yatwö clan. Böri elders at Kösumba gave me the genealogy of a truncated Yatwö clan with Duru'le as the founder (see Fig. 2). They confirmed the Lafon Lokoro statement that none of the Böri stock intermarry, though now very numerous and long ago divided. Visits are still made occasionally from Kösumba to Lafon, the waterless plain in between being crossed at Bödingölu swamp. The Nile Böri no longer speak their original language, but the observer is instantly struck by the identical appearance of Kösumba village, with its closely packed huts with high pointed roofs and homesteads which are often stockaded, and the villages on Lafon Hill. Such building is not typical of Nile villages, and the Böri at Kösumba claim to build as they did on the mountain. In Fig. 2, I give the genealogies of the three Böri groups.

iii. *Nile Mandari from the western peoples*

Clans which divided off from the western Mandari of Tindalu also live on the Nile. Their early founders have the same names as founders of certain Tindalu clans, and the migration to the Nile is remembered. Marriage with their relatives in Mandari is prohibited, but in fact they live too far away from them for this to be likely. Pressure on grazing drove some of them eastwards; others are descendants of 'soldiers of fortune' enlisted by an early Nile

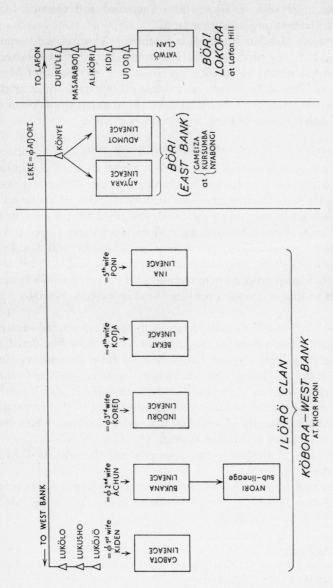

Fig. 2. All Böri groups as given by Nile Böri.

people to repulse invasion; these remained and married local people, later taking over their land.[1]

Western Mandari immigrants found the Tsera already established, but they preceded the Böri from Lafon, with whom they fought continually in an effort to retain their ownership of Moni Lagoon. They differ somewhat in physical type from river neighbours, and retain some Mandari customs; Mandari words occur in their dialect. None of them live on the east bank.

iv. *Independent indigenous lineages and immigrants*

There are other small Nile peoples. Some speak of coming at different times from Bari, Dinka, and elsewhere. Others say they are indigenous landowners (*komonyekokak*). Most of these have been oversettled by the groups already described. On the west bank, early landowners have land near Moni lagoon and larger tracts north of Terekeka. They call themselves 'Mandari', and may be a remnant of a once more widely spread Mandari people. Now they are only a small proportion of river-dwellers. Their position is analogous to that of remnant peoples found in western Mandari.

The Tsera and Köbora differentiate themselves from the western Mandari, while admitting that offshoots from those Mandari live among them. They suggest that the blanket use of the name originated with 'foreigners' (administrators and traders) and that formerly there was no contact between themselves and Tindalu Mandari (although the latter were known to live in that country). The Köbora, like the Tsera, had their own language, which has now degenerated into a Bari dialect.

Explorers of the last century support the distinctions I have mentioned.

Petherick seems to have crossed western Mandari on foot after having abandoned his attempt to reach Gondokoro via the Aliab

---

[1] River Mandari from Tindalu live as follows:

At the south end of Moni lagoon.

    Yukara clan.
    Mandari Böri—also called Mandari Rume having separated from Rume clan at Tindalu. They have no relationship with the Lafon Böri.

North of Terekeka.

    Ronkak clan.
    Lokweni clan.
    Tibari clan.

during the rainy season. He marks Mandari correctly on his map.[1]
So also does Emin Pasha, who writes of slave-raiding directed from
Rumbek and Ayak involving 'Dinka, Atwot and Mandari'.[2]
The Tsera (spelt Tshièrr) on the Nile were visited in 1840 by
Werne, who took part in an expedition directed by the Khedive.[3]
Werne describes the different Nile populations in some detail:
'South of the Èlliabs (Aliab) we came to negros who have a different
language to that of the Èlliabs, called Tshiérr.' He comments that:
'the shore is entirely covered with houses and cheerful cultivation
of Dura, simsim, tobacco and lubien.' He also mentions repeatedly
the vast herds of cattle, the large population, and the big villages,
one of which he describes with astonishment as having five hundred
huts. Werne writes of villages named 'Djar', 'Bamber', and 'Buko',
which correspond to the present day Tsera villages of Diar, Bam-
bari, and Bukö. He was also given reports of the 'Berri' (Böri) at
Lafon. He rightly assessed the relationship between the west bank
Koböra and what appear to be the east bank Böri (these he speaks
of as 'Lienns', probably referring to one of their lineages)—

At first sight of the morning dawn we heard the great wooden kettle
drum sounding opposite in the large village of Karborah . . . the watch
houses of the cow herdsmen stand in the centre of the enormous herds. . . .
The tribe of the Karborah . . . are a branch of the Lienns and independent. . . .

After 1900 there is little selective material on different Mandari
populations, although the Mandari are referred to, usually without
qualification, in writings on the Bari.[4]
When Mahdist rule succeeded Emin Pasha's withdrawal from
Lado in 1885, the western Mandari and the river Koböra and Tsera
suffered enormous losses in people and cattle. The western Mandari were raided for slaves and cattle from Ayak and Amadi, the
river-peoples from Gondokoro; famine and epidemics followed on

[1] Petherick, *Land Journey Westwards of the White Nile from Abu Kuba to
Gondokoro*, a paper read 25 April 1864 (R.G.S.).
[2] *Emin Pasha in Central Africa*, being a collection of his letters and journals,
trans. by Mrs. R. W. Felkin, George Philip & Son, London, 1888.
[3] F. Werne, *Expedition to discover the Sources of the White Nile*, trans. by
W. O. Reilly, Richard Bentley, London, 1849, vol. ii, chaps. v, and vi.
[4] Edited by L. F. Nalder, *A Tribal survey of Mongalla Province*, International
Institute of African Languages and Cultures, Oxford, 1937, pp. 139–41; A. C.
Beaton, *Equatoria Province Handbook, 1936–1948*, Sudan Government Publica-
tion, 1949, and various articles on the Bari in *Sudan Notes and Records*.

these events. The period is still spoken of as 'the despoiling of the country' (*kurju na kak*).

The Sudan Government Administration was established early in this century, but up till the 1920's it mainly took the form of a military occupation with army and police posts. In the early 1920's chiefs' courts, based on the old assemblies of elders, were established. A. C. Beaton says: 'local courts were established on the East Bank of the Nile in 1921, and, on the West Bank, by 1929 the system was well under way in all Mongalla Districts'.[1] Even so, some areas continued to be more thoroughly administered than others.

Details of the peoples called 'Mandari' living on the Nile have been included in order to distinguish them from those Mandari living inland to the west, and to elucidate to some extent the confused picture which confronts the visitor. Only the western Mandari in the inland country will from this point be described. There is no intrinsic reason why the Nile Tsera and Köbora should be included with them rather than other closely related neighbours like the Nyangwara. All these Bari-speaking offshoots have cultural affinities. To try to describe the Mandari and the Nile-dwellers together would add further complications to an already confused picture, while constant cross-referencing and qualification would be necessary. The Nile-dwellers have an economy based on living along a large waterway, and consequently are relatively static and closely concentrated. The Mandari are dispersed round about small rivers and marshlands dotted all over their country, and move continually.

It must be remembered, however, that the Nile Tsera and Köbora are more akin to the Mandari than either are to the Bari. All Mandari stocks are pastoral and all are more or less territorially isolated. They form a block of northern quasi Nilo-Hamitic cattle-keepers who are orientated towards cattle-keeping Nilotics. The Bari tribes now retain few cattle and are mainly cultivators. They are in closer contact with Arab and European influences and live nearer to or in urban centres. Many have become Mohammedan or Christian and are wage-earners.

The western Mandari speak a Bari dialect sufficiently unlike Bari to make conversation between members of the two tribes difficult. Their dialect is again distinct from that of Köbora and Tsera. A Mandari man who came with me to the Nile said he found it hard

[1] A. C. Beaton, op. cit., p. 14.

to flirt with Köbora girls because he often could not follow what was said; the Tsera dialect is likewise described by neighbours as 'like the language of birds'. During my time on the Nile I worked entirely through Bari-speaking Mandari. Bari is the lingua franca of the Nile and is used southwards from this point.

I now describe the country and mode of livelihood of the western Mandari, whom I shall simply refer to from now on as the Mandari.

II

THE MANDARI

Demography and Mode of Livelihood

I

MANDARI-LAND is a flat, ironstone plain, subject to serious drought for many months of the year. It is not badly flooded in the wet season, because soils tend to be light loams or sandy, but as the rains advance streams overflow their banks, and water is held in low-lying land and sedge swamp until well on into the dry season.

The vegetation is of a mixed, deciduous, broad-leaved, woodland character: the shady woodland trees—shea-butter, ebony, 'sausage' tree, mahogany, and other indigenous trees—growing among smaller acacia, thorny shrubs, and tall perennial grasses.[1] Around the villages constant clearing for cultivation has modified the thicker woodland, creating open park-like stretches of country dominated only by shea trees. In the rains, when the vegetation is a brilliant green, the landscape is pleasing. Small ironstone outcrops occur in some places; the largest, Mount Tindalu in the east, is a long shoulder of piled-up rocks, bush-fringed and topped by huge boulders. Its historic associations give it great importance to the Mandari. The soil here is more sandy, supporting mixed acacia, shorter thorny scrub, and fewer large trees than the red loams of the west. Further eastwards the poor, waterless soil of the boundary plain begins.

Over the whole country there is an acute shortage of the sedge swamp which provides grasses suitable for permanent dry-season grazing, and for about six months of the year the country has a cracked, sunbaked surface, blackened with burnt-off stubble, or covered with miles of dried-up, wispy vegetation.

The starkness of their pastoral life has made the Mandari a tough,

---

[1] Shea-butter tree (*Butyrospermum Niloticum* Kotschy), Acacia (*Acacia sieberiana* DC. and *Acacia campylacantha* Hochst.), Mahogany (*Khaya senegalensis* A. Juss), Ebony (*Diospyros mespififormis* Hochst.), 'Sausage' tree (*Kigelia aethiopica* Decne).

independent people, with an economy reduced to absolute essentials. Pride in their land, and harsh life, their isolation, and a tendency to despise peoples immobilized by material possessions or tied to agricultural economies, have made them, on first contact, reserved and wary. They themselves explain their toughness as resulting from the hardness of their life. Anyone, however, who spends some time in their camps and villages is the recipient of a hospitality and generosity which is both a traditional attitude to the guest and a genuinely spontaneous kindness. The diversity of their origins is admitted by them to be the result of their readiness to receive and establish strangers and destitutes, who have continually been settled on land and absorbed into communities by marriage and the system of Mandari clientship.

II

The Mandari have always been pastoralists, but the political upheavals of the last century, followed by epidemics among herds, and famine, and dispersals of owners, drastically reduced their cattle, which are only now beginning to reach substantial numbers. The fact that goats, hoes, arrows, and food were handed over in the marriages of the senior living generation has led to the suggestion that the Mandari were originally agriculturalists who recently acquired cattle. This is not correct: their economy was always cattle-based, though cattle were differently distributed from the way in which they are now, having been held by the landowning dominant populations, whose dependants usually cultivated the ground and kept only sheep and goats. The Mandari, in fact, speak of having taken extensively to agriculture in order to support life after the loss of their cattle. Herds were later slowly rebuilt, and augmented by trading ivory, giving girls in marriage to the Aliab and Atuot, and exchanging grain for cattle with them in times of famine. The average bride-wealth is now about ten head of cattle; many people marry for less, some for more. Higher payments are received, up to twenty to fifty head, from the Aliab Dinka, for beautiful girls. These wealthy marriages ensure wives for younger sons and are the basis of entry into Dinka grazing-lands. The Aliab favour them as a source of cheap wives and because the husband's relatives can visit, and 'eat off', Mandari in-laws during periods of short supply: moreover they wish to use Mandari wet-season grass. Girls are sometimes

averse to these marriages, since they feel homesick in the inhospit-
able Aliab country, where conditions are harsher, and where women
are expected to build huts and cattle-byres—work which is done by
men in Mandari. Different customs relating to marriage-cattle
also give rise to continual litigation between sets of in-laws. However, intermarriage, although bringing its own problems of social
readjustment, has formed the basis of the new economic co-operation between these two traditionally hostile peoples, who still have
to overcome, to some extent, mutual dislike and suspicion because
of a greater common economic need. Each must now contend with
the claims of in-laws and maternal relatives from another tribe as
well as those from other parts of their own country. Inter-tribal
alliances have promoted new stresses and tensions, and possibly, in
Mandari, which is much the smaller country, have led to some
loosening of exclusive units. Mutually ambivalent attitudes have
also exacerbated squabbles over grazing. Attempts to deal with
these have led to the formation of regularly convened government
courts attended by Mandari, Aliab Dinka, and Atuot chiefs, where
complaints are investigated and settled by new rates of compensation acceptable to both sides.

III

Milk and grain are the staples of Mandari diet, but neither is
sufficient alone, in the quantities available, to maintain health or
even survival. Each supplements the other in the total annual food
supply. Milk is the basic food only of the young unmarried people,
who are primarily responsible for taking the cattle to distant dry-
season pastures—although when camps are near villages for short
periods during part of the rains, milk is more widely available. As
the dry season advances, people try to leave some cattle at water-
points near home when the main herds are away. But in some places
this is impossible during the low-diet months, since both water and
grazing are exhausted, and villagers live almost entirely on cereals.

People in camps supplement milk with occasional fish and meat;
cattle are also bled in rotation. When milk is plentiful this diet produces good health. Some people, however, have no cattle, and herds
are continually subject to plagues. They are also reduced by the
social demands on stock that arise from marriage payments, compensation, and sacrifices made during illness and at death. Thus no

family can exist on its herds alone. A proportion of the population is based on the villages for the whole year, and cultivation is undertaken to provide alternative and supplementary food. The Mandari, having fewer animals but better land, grow more crops than do their Nilotic neighbours. They plant sorghums, several varieties of millet, cow-peas, beans, ground-nuts, and sesame; some maize, cassava, pumpkins, and marrows. Tobacco is planted according to inclination.

Horticulture is based on the mixing of a leguminous crop with millet, sorghum, and sesame; and mulching with hoed-up grass and leaves, which are left to rot on a newly turned-up field to provide humus, before it is sown with pulses. This pulse field is added the following year to the mixed-grain field and a new piece of ground is cleared for the pulses. When fields become sterile they are left fallow. Fields completely encircle the homesteads, and are themselves surrounded by uncleared scrubland awaiting cultivation.

Every elementary family has three basic fields which are prepared each time a man marries. These are:

(a) The ground-nut field.
(b) The mixed-grain field (sorghum, millet, sesame, and one kind of bean).
(c) The pulse field (beans and cow-peas).

Maize and tobacco are planted separately and homestead paths may be banked with cassava bushes. The amount of land each homestead has under cultivation varies with the demands of the homestead—the size of the family, the owner's social position (if he is a chief he must grow more than other people to meet extensive entertaining), and whether or not cattle are owned. The mixed-grain field, which is always the largest, may vary from under an acre to two or three acres. It is difficult to assess the size of the average field, as while the grain may be planted in one large patch, it is often distributed in a number of smaller patches round about the hut or outside in the bush. Grain fields never have a regular shape, partly because the Mandari say they like to see their fields straggling out into the bush from the hut, and also because the piece which is cleared each year for pulses is an extension of this field, which is then combined in it the following year. Ground-nut plots are smaller than the grain field, usually from about half an acre to an acre.

Forest plants, which spring up after the early showers in March or April, are collected, and help out the diminishing grain supplies until the maize and ground-nuts ripen. Great hardship can result if the rains are late, since planting and harvest are also delayed, and woodland vegetables are then no longer available. Roots, wild grass seeds, and tree fruits are also eaten, particularly the fruit of the shea tree, while oil, commonly known as shea butter, is extracted from the kernels.

Game and fish do not contribute regularly to Mandari diet, although they afford the occasional luxury. The shortage of fish is due to the scarcity of substantial lakes and rivers and the frequent light rains, which result in low water-levels. In good rain years, when the fish reach the swollen streams and lagoons, dams and traps are built or fish-poisons used. Fish are also caught in baskets by women while men work the shallows with fish-spears. Fishing is intermittent throughout the year, but is at its best by the end of the rains, when the high waters start subsiding and the fish can be trapped. During periods of hunger, hordes of women methodically comb stagnant pools with fish-baskets, hoping to catch small sprats that have been left by previous fishers.

During the rains herds of elephant, antelope, buck, and buffalo come back to the woodlands, and hunting parties are formed. Assistance is also given to professional elephant-hunters who seek ivory, in exchange for parts of the carcass. The Mandari only follow game for meat, and say that they do not bother to exploit other sources of woodland food intensively because they are 'people of cattle'. In the dry season game migrates to the Nile and is only found round the permanent Mandari lagoons of Mijici, Roro, and Mina.

Honey is a valued delicacy, and hollowed-out logs from which honey combs are regularly collected are placed in trees. Flying ants are trapped at swarming time and pounded into a relish.

The Mandari suffer less from hunger than do their Nilotic neighbours. They cultivate a wider range of crops and their soil is more varied, the sandy soils suiting ground-nuts and the red loams millet. Their natural woodland is also richer. In good years there may be a small grain surplus for sale to Arab merchants, and beads, cloth, salt, hoes, axes, spearheads, and even cattle are bought in exchange and hut-tax paid.

If the rains are poor it may be difficult for them to close the gap of four to six weeks before the harvest ripens. If the harvest is delayed in its turn, administrative assistance in the form of subsidized grain may become necessary. Famine will always remain a possibility as long as the yield of the fields is so small. Perennial shortages are also related to the difficulty of storing surplus grain, since the mud-and-wattle stores do not stand up to bad weather and the ravages of pests. Bulk storage in properly constructed sheds placed at strategic points might be a solution to this problem.

The delay or failure of the rains, cattle-sickness, grass and water conditions, and political friendships and hostilities determine people's economic activities in any one year. Life is always ultimately controlled by dependence on water, both on the village supplies and on the pools and streams in the woods and grasslands beyond. It is difficult to see how economic advance or the development of a more settled way of life can be attained by the Mandari until an extensive programme of deep-bore well construction has been undertaken. Men spend half the year following dwindling water supplies with their cattle, and women waste time and strength fetching water for the homesteads from pools, often distant and widely infected with guinea-worm. Drinking this infected water makes many people totally or partially crippled with sores for weeks at a time.

In spite of these difficulties, the Mandari are a cleanly people. Their huts and homestead yards are models of tidiness and order, and the women are good cooks in spite of the limited ingredients available.

Fig. 3 gives an approximate survey of the economic year.

III

ORIGINS OF MANDARI POPULATIONS

I N this chapter I consider the backgrounds and histories of the
main Mandari populations. This history is very important for
a study of present-day political relations, because it in fact
records the way certain groups of people moved around in the
past, who these migrating people were, how they regarded one
another, and the relationships between them which eventually
emerged.

Mandari-land has three different kinds of population, which
have been assimilated over the years. The first is the Bora stock; the
second, as far as can be known, is the earlier indigenous population;
the third is made up of groups of immigrants into Mandari who
have gradually, in certain places, succeeded in establishing powerful chiefdoms, often to the detriment of earlier occupiers. Mandari
is a country over which, and around which, people have been
moving constantly for a long time, and in doing so have either
reached positions of dominance, or gradually lost what they formerly had to others.

The Mandari invariably emphasize two factors in their history;
one is a group's original position as this is remembered in a myth;
the other is how this first position has been affected over a period of
time. For instance, two groups may know their original position in
relation to each other, one having been landowning and dominant,
the other in-coming, non-landowning, and dependent; but their
positions may have later been modified or changed completely,
members of the dependent group may have multiplied and assumed
a competitive attitude towards former protectors, sometimes to the
point of reversing the dominance situation.

Myths of origins, together with pseudo-historical statements, form

the theoretical basis of Mandari history and centre on pivotal ancestors who are claimed as founders of dominant landowning clans
which own the chiefdoms into which Mandari country is divided.
These ancestors are said by their descendants to have formed the
territorial and political divisions which remain important now.

1. The Bora[1]

The Bora stock who are established all over Mandari have a lot
to say about themselves, and their movements appear to have given
the country its political configuration. Members of the few remaining indigenous but non-Bora clans also confirm this Bora spread.
Bora people speak of coming from a place named Mandari Bora,
near Mount Tindalu. Their founder is never claimed as the first
inhabitant of Mandari, but as the one with whom the social and
political system came into being. (Before his coming, Bora myths
describe how death and sickness were unknown and the country
was largely treeless.) The past before his coming is forgotten, while
all that happened after it has a bearing on present-day experience.

Bora histories were given to me by elders of the following Bora
clans: Mandari Bora itself, Rume, Jarra, and Mijiki. Each varies in
detail, particularly as regards the name of the ancestor.[2]

Mandari Bora clan version

Long ago in the country of Bora there were people living. In those
days the earth was joined to the sky by a rope and the people of the
earth and those of the sky went up and down it in order to attend each
other's dances. There was no grass on the earth and no trees, neither
was there illness or death, nor pain at childbirth. The people otherwise
were very many, like the people of today.

One day two men fell to earth from Heaven.[3] They were Mar Nykwac
and Ruli his brother. A woman fell with them with a brush in her hand.
Ruli went back to Heaven, saying that the earth did not suit him, and
the woman followed. Mar Nykwac remained on earth and eventually
engendered two sons named Juŋdor and Mardesa. Their people lived

---

[1] Reference should be made to the map at the end of the book.

[2] Variation in name is to be expected, as it is customary for a chief to have
different names used indiscriminately. The two main ones are the birth name
and the one taken at installation. Elders pointed out to me that this was the
reason for the use of different names for the ancestor, but stressed the fact of its
being the same person.

[3] Some say they came down the rope; others that it fell with them.

in Bora country outside Mount Tindalu, where the rope was tied, and their old village sites can still be seen today.

The children of Mar Nykwac were many and began to quarrel among themselves. One named Juŋdor was a miracle-worker and warrior. He and his brother Mardesa went into the bush with their young men to hunt. Mardesa and his people suffered from thirst, but when Juŋdor saw that his men were short of water he made a pool out of a dried up water-hole by sweeping the surface with his arm; and all his people drank. Mardesa at last sent a messenger to Juŋdor to find out how he fared, and when he heard that Juŋdor had not called him to drink he was angry and sent two men to kill him. But Juŋdor escaped them in the bush. Mardesa then sent them out again but they could not trap Juŋdor. The latter then sent a messenger to Mardesa saying 'If my brother wishes to kill me let him come and do so himself.' So Mardesa came and threw a spear at Juŋdor, which went into his side. Juŋdor took the spear out of the wound and rubbed the place with his hand, and the injury disappeared. Then he asked Mardesa why he had tried to kill him without reason when he was his brother. And Juŋdor cursed Mardesa, foretelling that from the moment of his own death, trees and grass would appear on the earth, and death and sickness and suffering of all kinds would come upon men.

After three days, during which time he slept, Juŋdor died. Everything then happened as he had foretold, and for the space of a year everything on earth became barren: all women and female animals; and the men and male beasts were impotent, and people began to die.

When the people of The Above heard that Mar Nykwac's sons had fought, they sent a hyena to cut the rope, and the sky separated from the earth, and most of the people remained above. The descendants of Juŋdor and Mardesa began to separate out into groups, and eventually produced the following clans:

Jarra	Boreŋ
Mijiki	Bari Kujutat
Jokari	Rume
Lomore	Jungwa

Rume clan version

Long ago a man named Mar Nykwac fell to earth from heaven. His brother Ruli also fell with him, but returned. At that time there was no illness on the earth, there were no grass and trees, and the people were very numerous. The sky was tied to the earth with a rope, and the people of the earth and the sky attended dances together. Owing to fighting and the fear of blood between them, they decided not to see each other again. So the rope was cut by a hyena on the orders of the people of the sky.

Mar Nykwac married a girl named Are and produced Gumbiri, who in turn had two sons, Tokiri and Mardesa.

One day Tokiri, who was a wonder-worker, found a precious bead lying on the ground, which was invisible to Mardesa; the latter became very angry that he, as the eldest son, could not see it. He asked Tokiri to hand it over, but the latter refused, saying that he was the finder. So there was hatred between them. Then Gumbiri, the father of the ancestors, called both in front of him and told Tokiri to move to Dogomi country, to the side of Bora, and Mardesa to Reilly.

Mardesa produced the great-great-grandfather of the present Mandari Bora Chief, Janaba Lakule, and Tokiri bore various sons and his line ends in Fulai of Rume.

These stories relate the founding of the Mandari Bora and Rume clans. In one, Mardesa kills his younger wonder-working brother, in the other he engineers his banishment. In all clan versions it is Mardesa, the eldest son, who remains in the original homeland, his behaviour causing other siblings to leave or be sent away. In this way Mandari country is colonized.[1]

Jarra clan version

Jarra, another Bora clan, call the sky ancestor Jakda, and include the origin of burial and mortuary ceremonies in the myth.

Jakda (Mar Nykwac) was the ancestor. He came from the sky in Bora country. He had two sons Jundor and Mardesa. They went through the forest to hunt, and Jundor found good places where grain was ripening and there were pools, while Mardesa and his followers suffered from thirst. Mardesa was jealous of Jundor and sent his young men to kill him, and the latter went home to his wife and said, 'Come, we must flee because the people are coming to kill me.' But his wife replied, 'Are you afraid, that you wish to flee?' So Jundor waited and Mardesa's people came and threw spears at him, which passed backwards and forwards through his body from both sides, leaving holes through which light could be seen. But he felt no pain, and when his people came to mourn over him they found no sign of wounds.

A few days later the time came for Jundor to die. At this point the earth separated from the sky and grass and trees began to grow up. Death also came. Before that time there was no death. If people became old and feeble they were taken to the country of Jundor and laid on a frame over a fire on which medicines were burning. There they recovered, and went home.

[1] Fig. 7 on p. 56 shows Bora founders and their clans.

When Juŋdor died, he ordered his body to be buried in the ground and grave poles placed over it. From then on everybody has been buried in this way. Bonlek, a brother of Mardesa, also quarrelled with Mardesa because of the killing of Juŋdor. He left Bora country when Juŋdor died and settled in Jarra country, where his descendants are today.[1]

Mijiki clan version

Jakda, an important ancestor of Bora, was a miracle-worker. He had a chronic sore in his leg, which was never allowed to heal. He had a client whose duty it was to wait with an axe and every time the wound began to heal, to open it up again. Jakda never felt any pain or discomfort.[2]

At this time there was no death in the world, and Jakda spent his time searching for a seer who could foretell his death, but none was able to do so. In his anger Jakda slew a great number of male and female seers. Then one day a seer told him that if he caught hold of the tail of a cow named Keny and pulled it, it would kick him in the stomach so that he would die in three days. Jakda did as he was instructed and it proved a correct prophecy. He slept for two days and on the third he died.

At this time people began to die on the earth. The first son of Jakda produced Jarra, the second was called Amir and produced Mijiki.

We find the theme of a chief and his wonder-working younger brother with rain-power recurring in the Jungwa myth. This clan claims an earlier separation from Bora, and it is not clear whether the characters in the story are founding ancestors living before or after Jungwa moved away. It would seem that here the Bora myth had been grafted onto a direct Jungwa ancestor and does not refer to an ancestor then living in the Bora homeland.

Jungwa clan version

There were two brothers, Mar Gila and Gwonshuka. Gwonshuka was a miracle-worker; he used to take his cattle outside into the bush and sweep the ground with his elbow, and water and grass would appear in the scorched earth. His cattle grazed and drank all day and his people bathed. In the evening he returned to camp. His brother, on the other hand, took his cattle to the swamp in the usual way. One day one of Mar Gila's retainers followed Gwonshuka and, seeing all that happened,

---

[1] Somaring, an offshoot of Mandari Bora give Mar Nykwac his alternative name, Jakda. In their version he comes from the sky with a cow. He is also Jakda in the Mijiki myth.

[2] This sore figures in a fight between Bora and Koreŋ clans, see p. 31.

went back and told the chief, who became very angry, refusing to believe him.

Then the time came for cultivation, and the brothers prepared their fields. After Mar Gila had planted his, the rain fell in torrents, and continued all day on the fields of Mar Gila, which were utterly destroyed, and all the seeds washed away. No rain fell over these of Gwonshuka, and the people worked successfully and completed the planting. When Mar Gila saw what had happened, he remembered the story told by his retainer, so he trailed Gwonshuka and hid in a tree and saw the latter produce a fertile place out of waste land. In the evening Mar Gila returned to his village and found Gwonshuka lying on his face (because he was exhausted from having used his power) and he challenged him, asking why, if he had these powers, he had not helped his brother, and he said in a rage, 'You are not my brother', and cursed him. Then the latter said, 'How am I not your brother? Why do you curse me without cause? I will take my people and leave.' Mar Gila replied, 'All right, go.' So Gwonshuka called his people together with their cattle and families and left. They settled in Jurbeling, and his descendants still live there.

In a genealogy given by Jungwa, Gwonshuka is shown as the son of the founder, Bömu, who came from Bora. Further down the genealogy is a Mar Gila who, Jungwa said, was a grandson of the earlier one. In the following story, given me by a man of a split-off segment of Jungwa, named Bunja, Mar Gila is again a Jungwa ancestor:

One day a miraculous child fell from heaven in the centre of the camp belonging to Mar Gila. It fell by the side of a splendid ox with twisted horns which led the herd. When the people saw something dropping from the sky they came to look and found a small red bundle like a newborn baby, but without definite form or features. Then Mar Gila called his wife and she came to look, and it became a small, black baby with ears and eyes and limbs. She said, 'This is our child' and she brought the baby home, and though she was an old woman and past childbearing, milk appeared in her breasts and she suckled. The child grew and became a man; his name was Beksuk which means 'to peg down cattle'.

Lomore clan version

Lomore clan, who say that they were once part of Rume, validate their separation from this segment already split off from Bora with the following story:

There was an ancestor named Morjak who was a wonder-worker. For this reason his brothers hated him. When they were playing kandya[1] Morjak used to sweep the surface of the ground which became smooth. When he put the point of his elbow on it, holes for seeds would appear. Because of this his brothers hated him, so he decided to leave with his cattle and families. His huts and grain-stores went as well. The stores travelled in front, followed by the houses, and the cattle walked behind them with the people. When they wanted to rest, the houses and grain-stores sat down and the people spent the night in their home-steads. Eventually they came to the west of the country and found Wejur clan, who allocated land to them, where they stayed for some time, later moving on to Uguluma.

After the initial quarrel between Mardesa and Juŋdor, Bora fragmentation is seen as occurring rapidly. The Mandari Bora, commenting on this, say: 'We became many and were always quar-relling, so the father of the ancestors divided us up and sent those who were quarrelling with Mardesa to separate lands. The people were told where to go and given the names of their lands.' Groups divided off by the early founder re-divide and shift about. Their stories of movement are often variations on the theme of a younger brother with miraculous power who is hated by an elder one.

The significance of this mythical past for the present-day Bora clans lies in the fact that all their chiefly lines are believed to have links of kinship with the original sky founder and, therefore, a re-lationship of a kind to each other. Clan members also believe in many cases that their chiefdoms were directly allotted to them by the 'sky ancestor', who bestowed on the individual founders certain powers of a political and religious nature. These constitute a kind of divine charter for landownership (komonykokak) which, in turn, confers on Bora chiefs the power to perform rites for their land and rain (rain particularly, having been 'brought by Mar Nykwac with him from the sky'). Religious power, like chiefly office, is hereditary in most Bora lines.

During the dispersals, some Bora offshoots went eastwards from Tindalu to the Nile. A member of the Mandari Rume (Böri) living on the Nile told me how his ancestors were approached by a Nile-dwelling people and left Mandari to settle there.

Our ancestor was Nykwac, a son of Mar Desa of Bora. Long ago there was a great war in the Nile country. There was an important man named

---

[1] *Kandya*: a Mandari game. Holes are made in the ground to represent cattle byres; the seeds of the 'heglig' tree (*Balanites aegyptiaca* Del) are used for cattle, and one player tries to capture the herd of the other.

Lukupö. (No one knows what his clan was or whom the fight was between.) Lukupö had heard of great warriors in Goroŋa (the Nile name for Mandari), so he went to Mar Desa of Bora and took offerings of salt. One head of salt was very tall, the other smaller. On arrival, Lukupö found the special client of Mar Desa, Lupöyu, a great man of rain and shea trees, who was later buried with Mar Desa. Lupöyu said, 'wait till the drum beats and all the people come to dance, then state your case'. When the people were collected, Lupöyu presented the heads of salt. There was much dancing and feasting, and Nykwac was very impressed with the salt and said that he was willing to go to the country of Lukupö and help him in his battles. He took his cows, wives, and children and settled in Dingiri. Lukupö was delighted to have his assistance, and when Nykwac arrived brought his small daughter forward to slaughter in his honour. Nykwac, however, wishing to spare the child, said, 'Let her be my wife; and kill a bull for me instead.' But the child replied, 'Never mind. If my father wishes to kill me, let him do so.' Then she took a branch of a tree named Nuluti, which separates into small branches and has many leaves; presenting it to Nykwac, she said, 'Your clan will multiply like this.' She took a branch of a tree called Lugwörti, and handing it to Lukupö, said, 'Your clan will die out; and if a child is born with a large *kapulet* it will die; if with a small *kapulet*, it will live.'[1]

Then she was killed, and at the moment of her death war broke out near Nyangwara. Nykwac and his people scattered all the enemies, who fled. Nykwac took their grain stores, houses, and cattle, which he brought home. Then Nykwac was shot in the breast and died. His clan is now Mandari Rume. The clan of Lukupö has died out.

Although they are of Bora stock, Mandari Rume on the Nile speak of having separated from the Rume rather than from the Mandari Bora.

The Yuköra, another Nile Bora offshoot from Tindalu, speak of 'following a bull' and finding unsettled land.[2] They stayed for the river-grazing, and consider themselves to be the owners of part of the Moni lagoon. Three small clans, Tibari, Ronkak, and Lokweni, also say that they came from Rume to the Nile by 'following a bull'. They speak of being owners of land north of Terekeka, the Tsera clan of Bukö having come and settled with them. As can be seen from the map at the end of the book, the Bora are scattered in all parts of Mandari and have migrated beyond it to the Nile.

[1] *Kapulet*, the Mandari word for the umbilicus. In some children it is distended, owing to rupture at birth.
[2] 'Following a bull' symbolizes searching for new grazing.

Apart from their pre-eminent claim to ownership of land, other early clans consider that they were contemporaneous with them, or even earlier, and have similar ownership rights. Their title is conceded by the Bora, and at Tindalu I was given a Bora story of pre-Bora settlement:

In the days of Mar Nykwac's fall there was no mountain in Bora country; the place was a sedge swamp and people were living near. We do not know who they were, and most of them are now dead. One day, when they were in the swamp watering their cattle, a mountain was seen coming towards Bora in the sky. As it approached and saw the people in the swamp it called out and said, 'Get out of the way, get out of the way, I want to come and sit down in the swamp.' But the people didn't listen. So the mountain came and rested on the swamp and the people and the cattle were crushed. The swamp disappeared except for one small water-hole, in which water is always found even at the height of the dry season. The mountain is also full of fresh springs. The people who were killed became baboons, and their descendants can still be seen on the mountain today.[1]

There is no attempt to suggest that small indigenous groups living round Tindalu, which have been absorbed by the Bora and dominant incomers, are descendants of these people. Rather, the myth indicates a general division of population between the Mandari who spread out from Bora and smaller earlier stocks. The Bora claim to have infiltrated peacefully among local populations and this is confirmed by the latter. Mar Desa of Bora, for instance, took in leviratic union the widow of a man of a lineage named Merya who had always lived at Tindalu. Ako, Mar Desa's son by this woman, moved back to his mother's country at the foot of the mountain when the Bora began to divide up. Somariŋ clan, of which the present administrative chief is a member, are his descendants.

11. *Indigenous Peoples*

Other powerful groups were already occupying Mandari simultaneously with Bora and claim a similar landowning title. Böndöri-Nyayo ('to make others tremble') had land in two places, outside Tali and at Atit on the Atuot boundary.[2] Böndöri's land later became over-settled by non-Mandari immigrants.

[1] The water-holes and spring are still used.
[2] The land division of Böndöri came about because the cow of one ancestor

Wejur and Lorogak clans also owned different parts of the sedge swamp and grazing round Tali, together with smaller lines called Pobi, Iom, Banyejur, and Jabeki. These formed a friendly association which reflects an early kind of co-operation between unrelated local groups, who defended strategic water and grasslands of which all made use. The Wejur, Lorogak, and Böndöri-Nyayo no longer intermarry, having much earlier exchanged women in marriage to the point of becoming 'as one man' (like agnates who do not marry and whose interests are mutual). Disputes between them were settled by arbitration. Voluntary political co-operation often existed, formerly, between such small neighbouring groups; it helped to secure equitable distribution of grazing, and held back, anyhow for a time, the encroachment of powerful incomers.

In the course of time all of the above, except to some extent the Böndöri, were engulfed by immigrants from other tribes to whom they gave asylum and who later over-ran them. If, as would seem likely, these individual clans dotted about Mandari formed the original stock, most of them speak of their decline as beginning with the arrival of non-Bora, non-Mandari outsiders. The Wejur received a fugitive from Kic Dinka named Dimu. His descendants produced the Jabour clan, which holds an administrative chiefship and is numerically far more powerful than the Wejur, whose land is included in present Jabour country. The Wejur remain 'owners' of the land, and when the annual fishing season opens they present some of the catch to the police at Tali Post, whom they describe as their 'guests'. They no longer perform rites for their land, because much of it has been alienated by encroachment.

The Lorogak, who 'own' the other side of Tali, said that their ancestor, Kidi, came from the sky, bringing a breeding bull on to the sedge swamp at the back of what is now Dari summer grassland. Over the years they gave away land. The first settlers with them were Dari from Lugbara in Uganda, under their migration leader Mar Lubukak. He was befriended by Wöju of Lorogak, and together they discovered Roro sedge swamp after following Wöju's breeding bull, which wandered away from the main herd every day, to return at nightfall covered with wet mud and grass. Dari are now settled on the north part of Lorogak land and on Roro.

produced a succession of female calves, while an elder brother's produced only males. The latter accused the former of bewitching. Bad feeling led to separation. The younger, Sukuri, settled at Atit.

The next incoming group were Mokido, who were fleeing from famine in the neighbouring Moru tribe. They received land from Deju, Wöju's son. Subsequently Jokari, separating from Boreŋ of Bora, arrived 'very tired and hungry from the road'. They also received asylum. Later Lorogak fought a series of costly wars with the Aliab Dinka, which left few survivors, the fatherless children being 'brought to adulthood' by Mokido, who largely replaced them. More recently Dari, gaining in power and numbers, began to press their former protectors for more land for their growing population, while Jokari raided Lorogak cattle. Now Lorogak retain only the land immediately surrounding their village.

Other early landowners were Nyarkiteŋ, who lived in what is now Boreŋ country. They befriended the people who, having left Mandari Bora-land, later became Boreŋ. Nyarkiteŋ's ancestor had a cow with a forked tail 'which fell from heaven'. They later fled their country after losing a rain-spear which had been 'brought down from the sky' by Mar Nykwac, founder of Bora, and given to the Boreŋ leader after he left Bora country. The Nyarkiteŋ dispersed in several directions, and one part reached the Nile, where a Nyarkiteŋ line own Gigging water at the north end of Moni lagoon. They also told me of an ancestor Atiŋ, who owned a cow with a forked tail. Another branch went west and settled near Tali and became owners of Mina river.[1]

The Boreŋ migration was given further assistance on arrival by Laŋe, who lived next to Nyarkiteŋ, while, they claimed, 'the earth and the sky were close together and before Mar Nykwac came from the Above'. Boreŋ leader Wöji settled with their head Mareŋ Koka, while Wöji's son and his people stayed with Koka's son, Alimbek. Lokulya clan were also, at this time, in Boreŋ and affected by the Bora arrivals.

Other small groups are described by Bora elders as 'having come out of the bush' and affiliated themselves to their newly arrived peoples. One such is Malari, who joined Mar Böjönö, son of Tokiri of Bora and founder of Rume. Rume held that Malari could not be considered true landowners (*komonyekokak*) because they were roaming in the bush without performing the land or forest rites of ownership. Wörigöri and Tija, on the eastern flank of Mandari,

---

[1] The Nyarkiteŋ were interested to hear news of their divided lines elsewhere, each group saying that half of the people had gone 'westwards' or 'eastwards' respectively.

were over-settled by Gworoŋa, pastoralists from Fojelu, a Bari tribe. Previously they had lived under elders, cultivating and hunting elephant and selling the ivory to itinerant Arab traders to buy sheep and goats. The Gworoŋa arrivals bought the ownership of the shea trees and the forests from Tija in exchange for cattle. At Tindalu, Mayar have long been affiliated to Somariŋ clan of Bora.

The problem which seems to have faced all the early, small, dispersed, and unrelated landowners was that of accommodating migrating peoples or small groups of what were originally dependants, who in time increased in numbers, while their patrons, for reasons that are obscure, declined or even died out. There must have been sparse pre-Bora settlement all over Mandari, particularly round Mount Tindalu and the two channels of Tali River and its grasslands. The Bora themselves do not seem to have been the main cause of the pressure on these early groups, but rather other arrivals from all over the place, who began to flood into Mandari— a small territory sandwiched between powerful peoples. This supersession of old landowners by later comers, which can lead to explosive situations today, puzzles the Mandari. For the later incomers it represents the natural result of their growth and vigour. When they swamped their patrons numerically they needed more land, and their new equality was manifested in a desire to act independently and, if they wished, aggressively. Their former protectors consider that this shows ingratitude.

The process of reversal of roles seems to have been gradual, beginning with the voluntary handing over of spare land for individual settlement. But even with eventual absorption, each group retains the knowledge of its original position *vis-à-vis* the others, a knowledge which is still related to its present status.

III. *Immigrant Peoples*

The politically powerful clans descended from outside migration leaders are able to state who they originally were, and often the reasons for their coming to Mandari.

Two of them claim to have arrived in Mandari in numbers. These have become increasingly powerful, in contrast to other individual incomers who live either as client dependents of earlier established landowners or on small tracts of marginal land of their own.

Dari clan

Dari clan own Dari chiefdom and hold the administrative chief-ship, which includes a number of formerly independent chiefdoms. Their founder, Malo, came from Lugbara in Uganda. Their migration was in stages. Malo's sons, Luban and Bilea, stopped in Nyangwara (a Bari-speaking tribe) where Bilea remained and gave rise to a clan living there. Luban came on and settled with Mandari Bora at Tindalu until his people were involved in the seduction of a Bora girl. Lubukak, Luban's son, then left and eventually reached, and settled with, Lorogak as I have described.

Mokido clan

Mokido, originally called Kulundo, were Moru from Madi Biti. They had links with Mandari, a Kulundo man having married a Mandari Bora girl. According to them, they came as follows:

Ako, an important man of Kulundo, had two sons, Mar Nykwac and Penga. They were a rich people, and Ako gave a feast and invited all Kulundo to eat and drink as they wished. Afterwards he addressed the elders, saying, 'Have we not enough food? Can we ever be hungry again?' All replied, 'There can be no hunger.' Then they decided to set fire to their grain stores. A widow spoke up and warned them that, if they did this, hunger would follow. But they would not listen. So, to preserve her food, the widow played a trick by lighting a heap of rubbish behind her hut. When the people saw the smoke they cried out, 'the widow has fired her stores', and ran to fire their own. Then hunger swept the land and everyone moved with Mar Ako to Dari and were fed by the great-great-grandfather of Dari and by Lorogak. In the country besides were Jokari Pobi. All these clans formed a pact of friendship and agreed not to intermarry for a time. Later fierce struggles broke out. Mokido and Jabour tried to push back Wejur and Lorogak and take Tali river and grazing, but failed. Mokido means 'to hug the breast with hunger'. Other Kulundo descendants live in the original Madi Biti homeland.

Koreŋ clan

Koreŋ clan suffered a decline in power due to over-assurance, which led to migration to Mandari.

In the old days Koreŋ inhabited the country between Mandari Bora and Nyangwara. Koreŋ fought with the Nyangwara and were strong and victorious, so the Nyangwara, who were famous for their magicians, bewitched them to bring about their downfall.

The Koreŋ chief, Mar Dare, went hunting with his men, and in the bush he found the chief of Mandari Bora lighting a fire to cook meat. So Koreŋ sat down beside him. Now the Bora chief had a sore which smelt very disagreeable, so that when Koreŋ followers smelled it they looked around saying ' What is it that smells like *makioro*? ' (the pungent excrement of a certain bird). The followers of Mandari Bora quarrelled with Koreŋ for insulting their chief and several people were killed in the affray. Afterwards they returned home, Mandari Bora saying to Koreŋ, 'Why, if you are so powerful, do you not fight fire? Fire is strong but you are a match for it.'

Now there was a great area of desiccated grassland because it was the height of the dry season; so Koreŋ fired it. Then they shot arrows into the flames and when these were finished threw in bows followed by spears. When their hands were empty they said, 'Let us extinguish fire with our hands.' They rushed into the flames and died, all excepting one man, named Lodugu, who had gone to a girl's courting-hut far from Koreŋ.

When the widows heard of their husbands' deaths, they also threw themselves into the flames and Lodugu, on his return, found only the empty houses and a few remaining widows. When the Mandari Bora heard that he had escaped, they sent men to kill him, but he eluded them in the bush and fled to Bura country of Mokido, taking the remaining widows.

The wife of a Bura elder, named Jöto, went into the bush to gather firewood and found Lodugu. She ran home and spread the news and the elders came out and told him to go. He refused, and called for a roof, which was eventually brought. Then he and his wives and the widows sat under it; their heads were dry but their legs outside were beaten by the rain. Lodugu then married a Bura girl and their people mixed with those of Mokido.

Gworoŋa clan

Gworoŋa have a separation myth found also among the Bari, Dinka, and Luo.

Gworoŋa came from Föjelu of Chief Goro Gurnu. The ancestor (name unknown) had two sons. The younger borrowed the elder's spear and went hunting. He speared an elephant, which made off with the weapon in its body. The boy returned and explained what had happened but his elder brother was angry and refused an offered replacement. So the youth set out to track the elephant. He was away three years, but eventually met a herd of elephants with their chief, who questioned him about his journey. The boy explained what had happened, and the elephant chief offered to help, telling him to wait until all the elephants were sleeping.

Then he called the youth to identify the spear. (Each time an elephant is struck it runs away and pulls out the spear with its trunk and these are all stored together.) The boy found his spear and returned home. After some months he arrived, but his family had meanwhile given him up for dead, and his wives had been inherited. One day, when he was threading his beads, the baby daughter of the elder brother, who was playing nearby, swallowed a bead. The younger brother demanded its return, refusing all substitutes. The child was eventually divided down the belly and the bead extracted. Then the brothers separated; the younger migrated to Panabang in Dinka, where he died. His name was Mendik. His son, Mar Yaro, later left there because of the mosquitoes, and after his subsequent death 'on the road' his people reached Mandari and found Tija, Gölöri, and Wörigori, with whom they settled. Later Wurabek, Jaro's son, married a daughter of Rume of Bora. Gworoŋa now form part of this chiefship. They remember their Föjelu link, and do not marry with their kin under Chief Goro Gurnu.

Important incomers who have built up or acquired political power, usually by infiltrating into the land of others, are always conscious of their historical past. But they can never be land-owners (*komonyekokak*) in the full sense of the word.

Indigenous but non-Bora landowners, even if dispossessed, have land claims which are universally recognized and usually qualified by a simple explanation, such as 'we were born from this land' or 'we gave birth to it'. Rights of prior occupation remain after political overlordship is lost, and when I visited non-indigenous or Bora-owned chiefdoms, their elders would often present to me an elder of a small landowning line living among them and descended from the original inhabitants. This universal knowledge of origins in relation to the actual distribution of present political power underlies some of the strained political relations of the present time.

The Bora myths are shared by all the dispersed Bora clans, and they serve to explain the foundation of their chiefdoms, some of which were established on land which did not in fact initially belong to them. Their claim to have 'come from the sky', would seem to indicate an arrival from outside Mandari, with concentration for a time in the east round Mount Tindalu before further advances were made into the surrounding country.

All landowning clans who held chiefdoms are able to show, by their histories, that they have a right to their territory. It is important to know where you come from and who you are, and not be in the position of having to say 'our ancestor came from the bush', which is the heritage of some client dependants, because this is also the supposed background of renegades, possessors of the evil eye, and witches. It also implies low social status. The Bora know that they have a special title to their land and are proud of it and are, besides, more numerous than people of any other stock.

Mandari statements about the past are a mixture of myth and historical fact. The claim, 'our ancestor came from Lugbara, his people divided out in Nyangwara, one part coming on here (Dari) the other remaining behind,' is an objective observation, verifiable in this case, although not in all similar ones. The claim, 'our ancestor came from the sky at the time when earth and sky were joined', is symbolic. The plain historical statement which may be supported by contemporary evidence seems generally typical of people who themselves admit to being later incomers. All Mandari history, however, contains exaggeration: people are presented as more powerful, better rulers, or more lavish entertainers than they are today. The kind of feats claimed for Bora founders are, however, recognized by the Mandari as being on a different level from, and beyond the scope of, ordinary human beings. These early myths tend to support important religious powers as well as political dominance, whereas historical statements are made in support of more recently acquired secular power, peaceful infiltration, and sometimes usurpation. An old landowner, when commenting on the frequent intermarriage between members of some groups of outside origin and the Atuot and Aliab, pointed out that the presence of strong Dinka influences among them were not surprising because they were 'anyhow not really Mandari'.

Every land-owning clan, whether operatively landowning or dispossessed, has its traditional history. But client lineages usually have little to say about their origins.

POLITICAL ORGANIZATION

IV

ADMINISTRATIVE DIVISIONS

MANDARI country was originally divided into a large number of independent village-chiefdoms, occupied by owning clans of one or other of the kinds of population just described.

The traditional boundaries of chiefdoms still enclose important spheres of partisan loyalty and social activity, despite the political changes that have recently been introduced. When the southern Sudan was opened up during this century, the administration over a period began to combine chiefdoms into larger units, placing each under a government-sponsored chief. Chiefs were chosen either because they were hereditary claimants from the most powerful of the units in the new combination or because they were, as individuals, considered suitable for office. There are now six administrative chiefships in place of the thirty or more chiefdoms which formerly claimed independent leaders.[1]

The Mandari seem to feel that these new divisions promote the interests of the administration rather than their own as they see them; and it is creditable in view of the diversity of the Mandari populations that the amalgamation of old chiefdoms should have been brought about relatively peacefully. It is, however, in some places definitely the cause of present stress situations. Relations between the old chiefdoms were often hostile and their interests were often divergent, and these rivalries can still lead to conflict, especially where enemy chiefdoms have been combined together in a single administrative unit. Some of the small groups now amalgamated, however, admit that they could not have remained indepen-

[1] The administrative chiefships are those of Dari, Bari Kujutat, Mokido, Jabour, Mandari Bora, and Rume.

dent indefinitely because of their lack of numbers and the pressure of powerful neighbours. Many of them were already in loose federations under their own leaders. These have now become inflexible political divisions with an element of hierarchical dominance.

The merging of the original groups was, no doubt, only possible because of the careful appointment of ousted hereditary leaders as sub-chiefs and headmen of the new administrative units. These former chiefs and the councils which assisted them have a changed and restricted political role, but they are still consulted in social, economic, and juristic matters. They cannot now take independent political action or settle major cases, which are periodically brought before the court of the administrative chief.

The traditional political boundaries, which enclosed exclusive spheres of influence, are still supremely important to the Mandari and their lives centre around them. Land divisions have not changed, and partisan loyalties, economic and religious affiliations, and inter-group relations continue to reflect and be conditioned by the old geo-political organization. Personalities whose forebears represented the past autonomy of a group continue to have influence even when lacking political authority. For this reason knowledge and understanding of earlier political segmentation is of great importance to present-day administrations.

My own observations while living in a number of these former chiefdoms have been augmented by information given me by elders and chiefs, many of whom were young adults before or at the time the administrative amalgamations were made. Some of these are more recent than others. The merging of Jungwa with Dari, for instance, took place only a few years before my visit, having followed on the death of the Jungwa chief, for whom there was no obvious successor. Jungwa, with whom the amalgamation was never popular, already talk of wishing to secede.

V

THE INDIGENOUS CHIEFDOMS

I

THE Mandari chiefdoms, which are still owned by the people who held them formerly as independent political units, vary considerably in size. Many represent little more than a dispersed village with its surrounding woodland and grazing, although a few cover relatively large tracts of land and contain a number of villages, separated from one another by woodland and grazing.

The compactness of the former Mandari political units, each confined within its territorial boundaries, cannot be too strongly emphasized. They bear no relation to the large, dispersed political units of the neighbouring Nilotic tribes. Again, the country is small and sparsely populated.

The land rights of a chiefdom are still jealously guarded by its members, and the transgression of rights over natural resources, particularly over water and grazing, leads to fighting. The boundaries of the smaller chiefdoms now often run together because unclaimed areas which are said to have been formerly buffer territory between chiefdoms have been occupied, during recent years, by peaceful expansion. Large-scale movements, such as those of the Bora, would be impossible today, and emphasis is placed on the thorough exploitation of existing homelands instead of expansion beyond their borders. The overlapping of the settled areas themselves is still prevented by the existence of uncleared woodland over which hunting takes place, and the Mandari attach great importance to this woodland screen around their villages. Thus the observer, only able to assess the different neighbourhoods by visible settlement, receives the impression that miles of bush separate one chiefdom from the next. The present precise definition of boundaries reflects the increase in the population and the tendency for residential units to spread instead of concentrating for easy defence.

Within a chiefdom, modified shifting cultivation is carried on. Families abandon fields after they have been cultivated for some five to fifteen years, and crop yields begin to fall off. The location of hamlets and villages gradually changes as people move to other parts of their land. Abandoned sites are left for long periods so that the soil reverts to scrubland. These former sites are pointed out as the disused hamlets (*roba*) of such and such an extended family. What now appears to be natural scrub often turns out to have been previously cultivated and to be set aside for future recultivation. Much of the country is secondary cleared bush. This accounts for a general lack of large forest trees, although a form of forest preservation exists based on the economic value of the shea trees, which are never felled.

A chiefdom belongs to the clan whose members are the descendants of its first settlers. These are spoken of as fathers or owners (*komonye*: fathers) of the land (*kak*).[1] There is a rough balance between the available land in a chiefdom and the size of its owning clan and their satellites except where this has been upset by oversettling, such as is found around the Tali grazing-lands, or where incomers have begun to crowd out previous occupiers. It would seem that the basis of all division has been spontaneous adaptation to the availability of land, though this cannot of course be easily demonstrated.[2] On the evidence it would seem that as a group increased in size it divided, and part of it moved away. A split became inevitable because the type of authority exercised by Mandari chiefs could only be effective over populations of a limited size. After this, stability was threatened. The precise moment when splitting occurred depended, of course, on a number of concomitant individual factors. The Mandari are aware of this process and describe it in a standard way: 'we became many and began to quarrel among ourselves; then we divided', a phrase which sums up the principle of all territorial and political segmentation.

There is as yet no shortage of land, and many formerly powerful landowning groups, now diminished in numbers, have retained the land they originally held because the ritual duties that are entailed by ownership cannot be superseded. Where traditional political supremacy is lost, owners may continue to live in a part of their country, retaining their landowning title, while other groups

---

[1] In Mandari the same word is used for 'father' and 'owner'.

[2] This point is raised and discussed by Dr. R. G. Lienhardt, in his essay on The Dinka, in *Tribes Without Rulers*, edited by Middleton and Tait. Routledge and Kegan Paul, London, 1958.

occupy other parts of it. Political power alone cannot confer 'ownership'. Although incomers of long standing sometimes attempt to take over ritual land duties, more often these lapse through mutual ill feeling. The breakdown of the correct connexion between a landowning group and its land, and subsequent quarrelling over the title to it, are given as a reason for bad rains and poor harvests.

Because of the religious responsibilities towards land, it is felt that the boundaries of chiefdoms should remain unaltered. Mandari Bora clans, particularly those living near their cradle-land, claim that theirs have remained unchanged since the mythical allocation of land; but in other less well-established chiefdoms it is recognized that changes have occurred. Boundary changes are seen as part of the slow struggle by groups of infiltrators to establish themselves among earlier established populations, some of whom were themselves on the look-out for new land.

The nature of landownership has usually prevented fighting for land, and there is no history of chiefdoms taken by conquest. Even Mandari Bora segments occupied outlying land peacefully, although, once they were established, fighting took place between some of their chiefdoms and those belonging to other stocks or even related ones.

There are few rules of land tenure within a chiefdom. When a family head dies the kin may continue to live and cultivate in the same place or they may move away, leaving that patch of land to be reopened later by people of the same lineage. The Mandari say, 'fields are only soil, they are not like cattle'. A chiefdom as a whole, with its recognized boundaries, is regarded quite differently; it is the relation between this well-defined area of land and an owning group which the Mandari envisage when they speak of *komonye-kokak*. This territory represents an intense complex of political, religious, and emotional attachments. People who have lost their homeland, or those who have come in from outside, are in a very difficult position because, having no 'country', they have no rights of citizenship. There is only one way in which their indeterminate position has been and can be resolved, and that is by client affiliation to a landowning protector which, in time, establishes social identity.

Dry-season conditions have always caused a proportion of the population of a chiefdom to seek water and grazing outside its boundaries, and in general the degree to which people move away from their specific territory depends directly on the amount of dry-season pasture available. Mokido, for instance, has no water or grazing by the end of the dry season, and almost the whole population encamps near pools on marginal grazing outside their country. In general, dry-season grasslands have always been exploited on a wider basis than that of the single chiefdom. They are used by agreement between the owning group and others, and formerly this sharing encouraged good relations or, at worst, watchful neutrality. The Mandari now augment their own grazing by that of the Aliab Dinka.

11. *The Landowning Clan*

The group of landowning agnates, which I call a landowning clan, forms the framework of each chiefdom. Chiefdoms have owning clans of different stocks, but all clans and chiefdoms have a similar structure.

There are two aspects of a clan. On the one hand it is a kinship group providing agnatic links between the main body of landowning kin in the homeland and individual persons or extended families claiming descent from the same clan ancestor but living in other parts of Mandari land. Between all these people marriage is forbidden and sexual relations are incestuous. On the other hand, a clan is an exclusive, territorially defined group of agnates living in one country, sharing political power and social rights and obligations, and having a common name and distinguishing features, for instance, its clan songs and drum. The relevant aspect of the clan concept changes with the social situation. The Mandari themselves recognize that their dominant landowning lines can be looked at from two points of view: they are both politico-territorial cores, and non-territorial groups of agnatic kin. When they speak of clan (*bay*) in connexion with their chiefdom, they refer only to the group of landowning agnates which has political and social solidarity and they do not, in this context, include dispersed kin. I use the word clan here largely in the way in which I believe the Mandari generally use it, that is, in its political sense.

As landowning title is based on living in the clan homeland, people who for some reason have moved away to other chiefdoms and settled with in-laws or maternal relatives remain agnates, but lose this title. They are living on other peoples' land where they have only residential rights. As clan membership in its fullest sense goes along with occupation of a specific tract of country, people leaving it relinquish, by so doing, some benefits of their member-ship in exchange for others, such as economic ones like herding or cultivating with a mother's brother. Complete severance of kin-ship, however, only follows from serious quarrels, or bloodshed within the agnatic group.

Thus, agnates dotted about over Mandari beyond the boundaries of their clan land, continue to fulfil kinship obligations to their homeland relatives such as attending mortuary ceremonies and marriage celebrations. After several generations of territorial separa-tion these may no longer be attended, and only the ban on marriage remains, and with the passage of time this may also cease to be observed. Should people who have moved away, however, return to the homeland, they automatically re-merge with the landowning group.[1]

A member of a landowning clan living as a settler in another chiefdom will say that in his present country he is 'a person from outside' or 'a stranger', but that his kin are landowners in such and such country, naming his original homeland.

While there is always some movement of population going on, the fostering of local kinship relations is an expressed ideal which is very important, since political relations are between localized chief-doms, held by groups of landowning kinsmen. But because certain individuals move away, families and even small lineages who come from other chiefdoms, are found in all well-established territories. They are attached to the landowners by some kind of kinship link and are important because they increase the group's strength by taking on new loyalties with their new residence, which, in time, supersede those that they formerly had in their homeland. Chief-doms also have affiliated dependants who are initially unrelated.

The landowning clan is patrilineal, and segmented within its own territory into named, landowning lineages.

---

[1] Separation and later reintegration occurred in Bari Kujutat. An ancestor, Könyuŋe Kitimar, migrated to Dinka but his people returned at about the same time the Sudan administration was set up. The chiefship was given to Mar Gayjuk of this line instead of to the senior line of Kujutat, which had stayed in Mandari. This is said to have happened owing to a 'misunderstanding'.

III. *The Pattern of Settlement*

In a large chiefdom with ample land the village of each landowning lineage will be separated from the next by woodland, in the
same way that, ideally, a chiefdom is separated off from its neighbours. By geographical dispersal different lineages stress their in-
creasing kinship distance. In small chiefdoms there may be only
one or two villages, and the lineages are separated from one another
by only small bands of woodland.

A landowning lineage, which varies in size from about fifteen
to over fifty adult males, lives in a chain of hamlets. Each hamlet is
under a family head, and the hamlets may or may not be sited con-
tiguously. Together they form the residential unit I loosely call a
village. Big villages have their own water supplies and grazing lands,
but small ones, composed of minor lineages or small landowning
clans, often share water and grazing, and their areas of settlement
are therefore more or less continuous. Certain parts of the bush
which are conveniently sited and regularly used by one lineage are
recognized by collateral ones as belonging to it. People who are
closely related try to keep together and thus establish moral claims
to convenient water, woodland, and forest, claims which are usually
respected since ill feeling results from disregarding them, although,
in Mandari theory, the land of a chiefdom is available for all its
members.

Homesteads are separated by tangled woodland, tall grass, and
fields of crops. The layout of a hamlet can only be clearly seen
when the dry-season grass is fired and the individual huts can be
espied between the thin trunks of woodland trees. A hamlet is
occupied by an elder, his married sons, dependants, and any
maternal or affinal relatives who have settled with them. Though
fathers and sons like to keep together (extended family ties are the
recognized channels of mutual assistance), they cannot always do
so if land is limited. Sons may be forced to break away and settle a
mile or two off in uncleared bush or, if there is no available land
round the hamlet, outside the village. They will then build a good
way off in order to leave room for a new hamlet to grow up around
them. Moving, therefore, means separation from the natal group
and having unrelated settlers, or in-law, or maternal kin of other
landowners as close neighbours. While in daily tasks new ties of
common residence result from mutual aid and entertainment of

neighbours, the closest ties are still with the near kin, left behind in the old hamlet, who are the people to whom automatic appeal is made in time of need. As younger brothers and cousins marry they are attracted to the new hamlet, and so a hamlet always has a nucleus of close kin although all close kin do not necessarily live together and kinship ties are augmented by those of convenience and friendship. This preference for branching out territorially rather than for the close settlement of a restricted area makes Mandari villages straggle. A man likes to see his fields spread out around his homestead, and those Mandari who have travelled comment unfavourably on the packed homesteads and well-defined villages of the Tsera and Köbora on the Nile.

Large, non-landowning, lineages who occupy land for building and cultivation do not have these recognized rights challenged by established owners, since they are not only usually affinal relatives, but also useful political allies and helpful neighbours.

Daily life centres round the hamlet. Mutual help is given with cultivation, building, roofing, heavy clearing of the uncultivated bush, and pasturing sheep and goats. This co-operation becomes apparent when the first rains break and related males begin clearing and breaking up the ground, working the fields surrounding each hut in turn. Wives and children subsequently collect up and burn the grass and weeds. When all the fields are ready for sowing, the individual owners plant and maintain their crops. The women co-operate in cutting the grain harvest and digging up ground-nuts.

If there is insufficient hamlet labour for a specific task men of the village are summoned. This labour given by more distant relatives or unrelated men should be paid for with beer, food, or tobacco; labour by members of a hamlet is given on a reciprocal basis.

The only economic activity which demands the co-operation of members of a whole chiefdom and of other chiefdoms is the dry-season herding of cattle. Smaller chiefdoms used also to co-operate to defend their lands or to exploit wet-season forest grazing and water. The small landowners around Tali river and grasslands and the fragmented groups in the west of Mandari towards Jamiŋa and Uguluma had land utilization pacts of this kind.

IV. Naming of Land and Kinship Units

The word *baŋ* is used by the Mandari to describe divisions of a chiefdom and segments of a landowning clan. *Baŋ* means a single elementary family, an extended family, or a lineage. It is also the word for a man's homestead, a hamlet, or a village. The implication is that the units of a territory are always occupied by at least a nucleus of people of common descent.

Baŋ is used in a looser sense for all the people inhabiting one chiefdom, many of whom are unrelated, and it can in this sense also refer to the whole Mandari people or their country. When it is necessary to distinguish between living together and being of the same kin group the word *jur* (country) is used for the land unit; '*Yi a jur geleŋ, naga baŋin kade*' ('we are of one chiefdom but different descent lines'). If *baŋ* is used for 'country', being of different descent can be conveyed by the word *yuŋi* (blood relationship), which includes kinship through either parent. *Kakat*, the word for a lineage (segment of a clan), and *jur*, that for a country, are specific as opposed to general words. The verbal identification of parts of an owning clan with the territorial divisions of its chiefdom shows the way the Mandari see the interdependence of these two kinds of segment. Proper names for both also mark their fusion. The owning clan names its territory or vice versa. For instance, Dari land-owning clan, near Tali, is divided into six landowning lineages, Woŋösek, Dakotiaŋ, Surukulya, Rokwe, Dari-Baŋ lo Are, and Kaŋgi which together make up Dari chiefdom. Each lineage owns the land on which its members live and so names it.

The origins of clan and land names are often known. Some are nicknames, such as 'Mokido', from *Mok*, meaning 'to hold', and *kido*, meaning 'the chest', which was given to the Moru group, Kulundo, who came to Mandari during a famine 'clutching their breasts and bowed with hunger'. Nyarkiteŋ are the 'cow-lovers'; Böndöri-Nyayo 'make people tremble', and Memede are 'those who are continually looking out for'—in this case, for marriage-cattle.

Small, non-related lineages attached to landowners often have the name of their founder's country tacked on to that of their host's line. Thus Jokari Jöŋö originated from Aliab (Jöŋö) and attached themselves to Jokari landowners. The name of the country of origin only may be used when founders are known to have come from other places and tribes. This explains why lineages called 'Bari', 'Fajelu', 'Korgi', and 'Nyangwara' are attached to dominant land-owners.

Clans are sometimes named after places or natural features,

although place-names are not usually important. Some old Bora clan names such as Boreŋ and Mandari Bora are said to have been place-names. When the Bora clan split, those left behind retained these names, and the departing segments used their own lineage names, or in time acquired new ones in their new country. Thus the senior clan in the Bora homeland still bears the original name, 'Mandari Bora'.

Lineages of a clan are often named after the natal line of a foundress, groups stemming from different sons being distinguished from one another by reference to their mothers. For this reason lines with the same name but which are not segments of the same clan are found in different places; the relationship between them is often that of a classificatory 'mother's brother', 'sister's son' kind.

The significant names are always those of the landowning clan and its segments, and no country is named after a client or outsider group which has rights of usufruct only. Small hamlets may be named by reference to client occupiers for convenience, but the names have no political significance, and indeed are rarely known at any distance. Exceptions are where former dependent groups have overrun their hosts, as in the case of the Moru immigrants, Mokido, who gradually assumed political power over their Lorogak patrons. Their chiefdom, which includes former Lorogak land, is now known as 'Mokido'. Wejur land, similarly overrun by Jabour, is now known as 'Jabour'.

v. *The Structure of the Landowning Clan*

To indicate the structure of a typical landowning clan I describe Dari, who although originally a non-Mandari group, have very ancient settlement rights and are to all intents and purposes now landowners.

Dari clan is made up of six landowning lineages (numbered 1–6 in Fig. 4). I call the levels at which they branch out from the main clan stem 'generation segments'. The founder of the senior lineage, Aloŋ, had few sons and grandsons, with the result that his line remained undifferentiated. Mar Dara, his younger brother, had five surviving sons all of whom had descendants, each group of which took a distinguishing name. Taking a name both reflects and stimulates a feeling of separateness, which is often strengthened by the geographical movement of the people away, at least from the

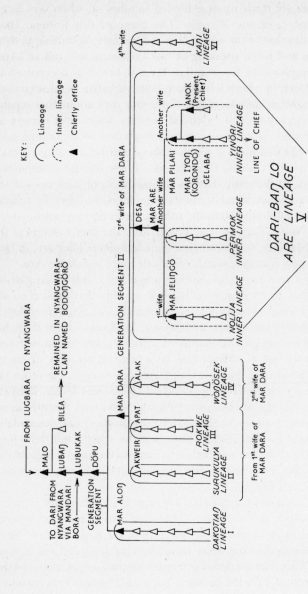

Fig. 4. Dari landowning clan.

same village. Naming and segmentation tend to be synonymous, and named divisions (lineages) are called *kakasi*.

Lineages are made up of extended families or, when very large, like lineage 5, of sub-lineages. The name of this lineage, Dari, which is also that of the whole clan and country, is starting to drop out of use and when speaking of this lineage people talk of 'Are', thereby emphasizing the founder Are, the begetter of twenty-four sons, eighteen of whom left descendants. Because the descendants of these eighteen men were also numerous they are further separated into three powerful extended families which still occupy an almost continuous settlement area, though they are beginning to be conscious of themselves as separate social entities standing a certain distance apart. While all three act as a single lineage in important clan affairs, in domestic matters the members of each respect the authority and seek the advice of its own elders, and thereby achieve a degree of autonomy from the others. Recently they assumed the names of Nolija, Permok, and Yinöri, after the natal lineages of the wives of Mar Are, who produced their founders. They are, in fact, potential new lineages, which could, in time, supersede Are.

Lineages are found in all landowning clans, but from an analysis of more than thirty clan genealogies it appears that most clans are not large enough, nor their lineages of sufficient generation depth, to redivide into sub-lineages. However, Mijiki clan, from Bora, has the same kind of rapid development within a single line as we found in Are (see Fig. 5). Mijiki has two main generation divisions, one descended from Mar Gayjuk forms one lineage, the other has four lineages which have separated off at different levels. Banyata, the fourth lineage of these, became very weak and recently amalgamated with Nyirom, the line of an elder brother. The descendants of the senior brother Mar lo Koka, on the other hand, now form two lineages, Kamana and Nolija, because of increase in population.

Most clans, however, divide into lineages from one generation level only (see Fig. 6).

The general absence of clan sub-lineages such as are found in Dari is, I think, accounted for by the small size of most landowning clans, and by the constant dividing up of the larger clans of Bora, their segments moving away from the clan land and losing their identity. This past tendency towards complete separation and dispersal conflicts with the present-day trend towards concentration, itself the direct result of the lack of opportunity for groups to move

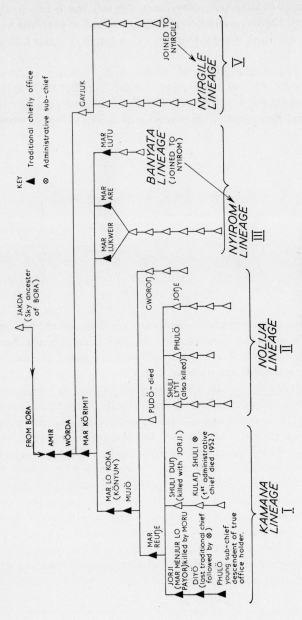

FIG. 5. Mijiki landowning clan.

about owing to shortage of unused open country and government disapproval of large-scale movement. The lack of sub-lineages is also related to the large number of lineages found in even the smaller clans, sometimes four or more in a clan totalling about a hundred males.

The genealogical depth of a clan usually averages eight to ten generations. The Mandari recognize the fact that early ancestors are always being dropped out. The first one or two are permanent structural points (often associated with a myth) who represent a

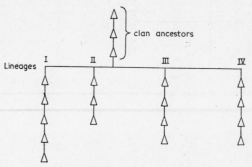

FIG. 6. Typical clan structure.

whole line of unimportant forgotten males. Key individuals cement the lineages together and enable each individual to know theoretically his relationship to every other clansman in the chiefdom, and recently separated kin in other places.[1]

A lineage may occupy a separate tract of land and be economically independent of collaterals except in the all-important matter of herding. Lineage elders settle minor disputes, and members of one lineage usually meet together for the performance of rites for sick members. The degree to which any particular one displays all these characteristics depends on its size, and in the case of economic co-operation, on the distribution of natural resources in the chiefdom. The identifying names are, however, always important; thus in Dari, neighbouring chiefdoms know the names of its six landowning lineages, but they would not necessarily know the names of the sub-lineages of Baŋ lo Are lineage unless they were, for some particular reason, interested. Politically it is always lineages which are significant, not their smaller divisions.

[1] It is in fact only senior clan members who are able to give the ramifications of clan relationship.

PLATE I

a. Fetching water

b. Group by ashes of cattle-camp fire

Because lineages which would in former times have broken away can no longer do so, many have evolved a greater internal autonomy. Dari themselves compared the relative concentration of their large lineages, which are only separated from one another by bands of woodland a few miles wide, with the dispersed lines stemming from the original Bora nucleus, which over a longer period, and with greater scope for movement, spread out so that the feeling of common identity was lost.

The evidence on which this analysis of clan structure is based cannot be presented here, since it consists of more than forty clan genealogies and histories collected both in Mandari and among the riverain Tsera and Köbora.

VI. *The Political Aspect of the Landowning Clan*

Within the chiefdom each landowning lineage is politically equivalent to its collaterals, regardless of its seniority as shown by the point at which it divides from the clan stem. In Dari, for instance, political power is shared equally between all six lineages, but the sub-lineages of Baŋ lo Are lineage are not political groups. The Mandari generally regard named lineages of approximately equal strength as being equal in other ways: a principle which is the basis of their whole political structure. Numerical balance in man-power is what is important from the Mandari point of view. Thus line I, which is also the complete generation segment I, being weak, never divided.

In situations which demand inter-lineage co-operation, lineages either combine in total, or two or more may join together as a situation demands. Combinations of lineages inevitably arise against pressure from outside the chiefdom, because combination in opposition to other groups within one country would lead to chaos. Thus the five lineages in generation segment II of Dari never see themselves as a political group in opposition to lineage I embracing generation segment I, and lineage I differs from the other lineages only in seniority. This would normally give it chiefly office, but in actual fact chiefship has followed the powerful Are lineage.

Chiefship unites all segments of the territorially defined owning clan, as well as ultimately claiming the loyalty of all members of the chiefdom however they may be related. Landowning lineages have a particular interest in protecting the chiefship regardless of their

E

position in the clan kinship structure. The internal balance of the chiefdom is preserved by equal representation under the chief at the central meeting-tree. The possibility of power being usurped by expanding junior collaterals is, however, recognized by the Mandari, who know that inequality in the size of landowning lineages has in the past led to the division of clans and to the moving away of some segments. The desire to gain independent power away from the parent clan has its place in Bora mythology, where division is seen as the outcome of conflict between 'brothers', who probably represented 'brother' (collateral) lineages, with ambitious men at their heads.

Large lineages like those of Dari clan, tend to act as independent units in social situations. At important mortuary rites, each is represented by its own elders. In marriage distributions and the payment of compensation, lineages may give and receive cattle on an equal basis. For instance, at the marriage of a daughter of a chief, or a powerful lineage head, if there are sufficient cattle to make a distribution of them beyond the immediate lineage kin, each collateral lineage will receive an ox. Thus when the daughter of Chief Korondo of Dari married a Dinka chief for a substantial bridewealth, heads of all collateral Dari lineages received the ox of a 'brother'.[1] Again when a man of Dakotiaŋ killed a Bor Dinka, collateral lineages contributed to the compensation when the offender's lineage and the lineage of the chief had produced the greater part.

There is often no direct correlation between genealogical distance and the territorial distribution of lineages. Thus in Dari, Are and Surukulya live about fifteen miles apart, while Dakotiaŋ and Are share the same land, though the former lineages are nearer to one another in terms of clan segmentation than the latter. The fact that geographical proximity tends to make people feel closer to near

---

[1]

Deŋlo Bugga—head of Surukulya lineage			1 ox
Möjut Awol	,, ,, Woŋösek	,,	1 ox
Mabour lo Ako	,, ,, Rokwe	,,	1 ox
Magok	,, ,, Dakotiaŋ	,,	1 ox

The following lineage representatives also received an ox each:

(a) Yoane, member of the part of Dari left behind in Nyangwara and descended from Bilea, brother of Mar Lubukak of Dari. Yoane, who is a medical assistant, was then stationed at Tali, and put in a claim for this animal. (b) Butis Agworong, head of Mandye lineage, affiliated to Dari through their female founder, who, after bearing a son by an unknown man, later married Dari chief, Mar Are.

neighbours than to agnatic kin living farther away never obscures the knowledge of the real lineage relationship. It is, however, the situations of daily life which tend to be emphasized, rather than arbitrary bifurcation points in the descent line, and importance may be given to territorial solidarity at the expense of agnatic kinship solidarity beyond the lineage. The history of Bora movements demonstrates very well this desire to form separate territorial and political units even at the expense of severing kinship.

VII. *Special Features of the Bora Clans and Chiefdoms*

I have described how the Mandari are composed of three kinds of population each of which is divided into clans which held chiefdoms. There are firstly the two kinds of non-Bora, chiefdom-owning clan. Only four sizeable ones remain of the indigenous population. None of them holds administrative chiefly office, but they occupy part of their old countries. These four clans are quite distinct, and say that they have no remembered common ancestor. Their chiefdoms therefore had no historical linking through their nuclear groups to other Mandari chiefly lines.

As regards the established clans of foreigners, some of these, notably Dari, Mokido, and Gworoŋa, have collateral lineages in their countries of origin of which they are aware. They would not marry these distant collaterals and would greet them as kin if they met, but in Mandari they have a position of historical isolation. As far as it is possible to ascertain now, the indigenous clans and the foreign landowning ones together accounted for about half of the old chiefdoms.

(a) *Early indigenous clans and chiefdoms.*

> Böndöri-Nyayo
> Nyarkiteŋ
> Wejur
> Lorogak

(b) *Foreign 'landowning' clans and chiefdoms.*

Dari	from	Lugbara
Jabour	„	Kic Dinka (or Böri, Nile)
Mokido	„	Moru
Buntuk	„	Aliab
Gworoŋa	„	Föjelu

Koreŋ   from   Nyangwara
Buju   „   Föjelu
[1] { Tumunuk   „   Föjelu (offshoot of Gworoŋa?)
{ Kwöröjidita   „   Bari (near Juba)

With the exception of the first three in list (*b*), who hold administrative chiefships, foreign clans own single-village chiefdoms in the west of Mandari, where they are mixed with small Bora offshoots.

Bora landowning clans had the largest number of chiefdoms and now hold three administrative ones. All are linked to each other ideologically across their territorial boundaries. This linking is conceived of in terms of their common descent from the founder of Bora. Their myths present each clan founder as a 'son' of this ancestor, and their division into chiefdoms is looked upon as having occurred at much the same time, that is at the big split when earth also separated from sky. The founders were ordered to go off by the 'ancestor', and in some cases they were specifically allotted certain parts of the country, a fact which justifies their present territorial, political, and religious power.

While early landowners of the non-Bora type also claim that they had chiefs similar to those of Bora 'at the time Mar Nykwac was ruling there', Mandari chiefship is strongly associated by Bora people with their own ancestors. I was told that the country is made up of independent chiefdoms 'because it was divided out by Mar Nykwac; then people from outside came in' and built up chiefdoms on the Bora model. Bora know and admit that divisions in their stock took place because of pressure of population, but they also stress the special authority vested in their first begetters to divide up, and separate out.

After the initial Bora separation further splits are claimed to have occurred, leading to the formation of other chiefdom-owning clans which are now independent of, and equal with, their parent ones. Jungwa, on the extreme north-east boundary, remember their Bora connexions but claim to have left before the separation and to be able to intermarry with other Bora. In actual fact, owing to their isolated position, they marry people from neighbouring mixed clans, Dari, Mokido, Jabour, other small lineages, and the Atuot. They also ally themselves for political and economic purposes with non-Bora peoples. It is admitted by representative elders, that it

[1] These two are only small lineages.

was only when Bora chiefdoms were territorially adjacent that compensation was paid for killings between them. (Peaceful settlement
was also a feature of chiefdoms of mixed origins living close
together.) There is a sentiment that Bora chiefdoms should not
fight one another, but fights in fact occurred even near the central
homeland. An example is the breach of relations between Mijiki
and Mandari Bora, due to the activity of a Bora traitor.[1]

Near Tindalu, Bora chiefdoms formed temporary defence alliances for the protection of their homeland. The Moru attacked
Bora from the south and west, while the Aliab, sometimes allied
with the Atuot, bore down from the north and north-east. Bora
also speak of repulsing the Azande. Wars to preserve independence,
as opposed to cattle-raiding and vengeance forays, were always
against non-Mandari peoples.

The Tindalu homeland and surrounding country remain almost
entirely Bora-settled. Mandari Bora live west of the mountain,
Somariŋ at its southern base, Rume to its north, Boreŋ north-east,
Mijiki to the west, and Bari Kujutat west again on the Tali road.
The names of the founding ancestors of each clan and chiefdom
are known to the others, and each is described as a son of the 'sky'
ancestor. Further outlying clans, some of which were formed by

[1] A man named Quet of Mandari Bora approached the Dupi (Moru tribe) of the
ancestor of Roba line, and asked for their assistance in killing Mar Jorji, a famous
Mijiki warrior, and his sons. So the Moru advanced in numbers as far as Ryöli.
The chief at that place, Lubudiaŋ, asked the assembled army whom they were
attacking and the Moru replied 'Mar Menjur lo Payor' (alias Jorji). Lubudiaŋ
said 'If that is so I refuse to co-operate, his people are related to us.' Then he
took his bow and shot the traitor Quet while the Moru army stood and watched
in silence. Lubudiaŋ then returned to his village.

More Moru advanced and this army arrived at Mijiki. When the villagers saw
them approaching, the children loosed the goats and sheep and took them into
the forest, and women and girls shut themselves in their huts while the Moru
attacked. In the fighting Mar Jorji was fatally pierced in the shoulder by an
arrow. When Nyirgile, a collateral lineage, heard this they assembled under Mar
Mole, their head, and came to Jorji's aid. They arrived to find Mar Jorji already
dead, together with his brothers, Shuli Duŋ and Shuli Ly'it (Shuli the elder and
the younger). Mar Mole was later killed and so were many of his followers. The
Moru then retired with loot. (Mijiki told me that at the time the Northern
Sudanese troops were stationed at Tombek, and the Moru withdrew because
they did not wish to risk a punitive expedition being sent.) Diyö, a younger son
of Mar Jorji, then a youth, was left and became Mar. All those killed, including
Mar Jorji and clients were buried in a common grave.

(Diyö became the last independent Mar of Mijiki which was amalgamated
with Jabor by the administration during his office. Mijiki have a sub-chiefship
held by Diyö's son who followed Kulaŋ Shuli (cousin of Diyö) after his death
in 1952. (See Fig. 5, p. 47.))

redivision outside Bora, are not aware of the name of the original ancestor, but claim descent from him and separation 'out of Bora'.

The ties of common descent of the close-knit central clans still received social recognition, while each was separate politically. Thus Somariŋ still do not marry into the agnatic line of Mandari Bora, Rume, or Boreŋ; Bora do not marry Somariŋ, but marry Rume and Boreŋ, whose land is farther away. All these clans marry Mijiki, as kinship has been 'wiped out' by 'fratricidal' bloodshed. The centrally placed exogamous clans eat together at sacrifices, thereby showing that they are all of 'the house of our fathers' (*baŋ lo Aba*). When they attend mortuary ceremonies for one another's chiefs they bring a bull, 'to mourn as relatives', and receive a leg of the mortuary ox. Kinship lapses when people cease to attend ceremonies where kinship ties are given clan expression, and younger generations start intermarrying after protective ritual has been performed.

Political and territorial allegiance to their own countries and chiefs have tended to stress the separation of Bora clans, while ties of common ancestry in their ruling lines draw them together. This conflict between territorial allegiance and allegiance based on agnatic kinship ties is inherent in all Mandari groups. It exists now in chiefdoms when large lineages are unable to break away, and therefore begin to form autonomous units within the homeland. If fragmentation away takes place, as among Bora clans, kinship ties gradually break down in the face of exclusive political and territorial interests. Thus outside the central Bora block the ideal 'Bora kinship' was swamped by developing rivalries, a situation which is reflected in the myth of division and dispersal of kinsmen by the founder.

In analysing the structure of the Bora units we appear, in the purely agnatic context, to be dealing with a single, widely dispersed clan of a Nilotic type, spread over a country among smaller, localized peoples. What I have called Bora 'clans' could be regarded as dispersed lineages of different levels of segmentation. In terms only of descent all Bora could be described in this way. But because of other factors that overlie agnatic kinship, and make a purely kinship criterion inapplicable to these wider Bora units, I speak rather of a Bora stock, made up of independent clans linked together by historical ties which are stronger or weaker depending on the degree of territorial separation. When clans are geographically close, various kinds of real kinship behaviour are manifested; these are absent when the clans are spatially distant from one another.

To speak of 'stock' rather than 'clan' in connexion with all Bora seems realistic for the following reasons. Bora groups are not smaller divisions of a Bora clan because no such clan exists. The common territory which was the basis of former cohesion has long since been outgrown. In the alliances of the past, Bora segments never fused into larger units, although they sometimes made temporary pacts. There is no specific Bora 'country' apart from the one small chiefdom of Mandari Bora clan itself. The idea of an original 'Bora' now only evokes a sentimental response. Bora clans do not think of themselves as forming a single unit. When asked their names each will give its own: for instance, Rume or Boreŋ, and add, if it seems relevant to do so, that they came *from* Bora. Bora people now think in terms of their own discrete clans and chiefdoms and only refer to the universal Bora concept if they are specifically questioned about it. It belongs to the past, and the significance of being Bora lies mainly in the religious powers that it confers and the support it gives to chiefly houses.

The decline of functional kinship in Bora is related to the struggle for territorial independence. Allegiance to a country and chiefly office reduces the effectiveness of kinship linking. Attenuated links must in fact be severed to preserve the equivalence of political groups. Bora clans in different chiefdoms can see themselves as political rivals while at the same time feeling closer to each other than to peoples of other stock. When they are territorially near one another their common ancestry is stressed by exogamy and other kinship observances.

Bora clans and the ways in which they are linked are charted in Fig. 7. Shown in squares are the clans of the first splitting which is supposed to have taken place in Mandari Bora itself. Names in circles show the clans formed as a result of separations from the first divisions (from a Boreŋ or Rume, &c., ancestor). These later divisions gave rise to units similar to but independent of parent ones. Their relationship to the parent is expressed in statements such as 'we originally came from, and divided out of, Rume or Boreŋ', as opposed to 'we divided out from Mandari Bora'. Links with parent clans may prohibit intermarriage for a time, but, as with the clans of the first division, intermarriage now takes place between some clans and those from whom they divided. Lomore,

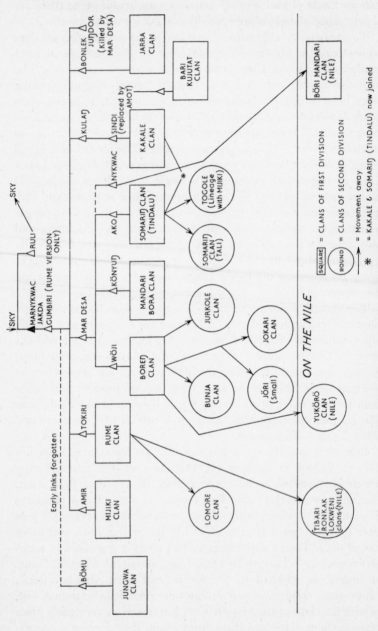

Fig. 7. Landowning clans of Mandari Bora stock.

SKY

MARNYKWAC
JAKDA
GUMBIRI (RUME VERSION ONLY)

RUU → SKY

Early links forgotten

BÖMU — JUNGWA CLAN

AMIR — MIJIKI CLAN

TOKIRI — RUME CLAN

MAR DESA

WÖJI — BORED CLAN

KÖNYUD — MANDARI BORA CLAN

AKO — SOMARID CLAN (TINDALU)

NYKWAC

KULAD — SINDI (replaced by AMOT) — KAKALE CLAN

BONLEK — JUDDOR (Killed by MAR DESA) — JARRA CLAN

BARI KUJUTAT CLAN

BORED CLAN — JURKOLE CLAN
BORED CLAN — BUNJA CLAN
BUNJA CLAN — JORI (small)
BUNJA CLAN — JOKARI CLAN

SOMARID CLAN (TALI)
TOGOLE (Lineage with MIJIKI)

ON THE NILE

LOMORE CLAN

YUKÖRÖ CLAN (NILE)

TIBARI RONKAK LOKWENI clans (NILE)

BÖRI MANDARI CLAN (NILE)

SQUARE = CLANS OF FIRST DIVISION
ROUND = CLANS OF SECOND DIVISION
→ = Movement away
* = KAKALE & SOMARID (TINDALU) now joined

split off from Rume, still do not intermarry with Rume but do marry Mandari Bora and Boreŋ. Jokari do not marry Boreŋ, from whom they divided, and Somariŋ do not marry two of their split-off segments, Somariŋ (Tali) and Togole; Jöri, a small Bora fragment, have an exogamous relation with their parent group Jokari. There are, therefore, cases of inter-clan exogamy based on remembered close ties. Ties are very weak when clans have split twice. Thus while Lomore cannot marry Rume, from whom they split off, they do marry the clans of the original Bora separation, such as Boreŋ and Mandari Bora. While the relationship between the founders of the Bora clans may be idealized as having been one of brotherhood, it is brotherhood of a different type from that which exists between lineages descended from true or half-brothers of a single, landowning clan in a chiefdom. When Bora clans claim such relationship they are aware that they are using 'brotherhood' in a special sense.

The importance of a Bora heredity is related to the mixed character of the Mandari population; if the country was wholly settled by Bora there would be no need to emphasize it.

Bora clans which owned chiefdoms were as follows:

(i) *Those of the primary splitting up 'in Bora'*

Mandari Bora	Jarra
Rume	Bari Kujutat
Boreŋ	Mandari Böri (Rume)—on the Nile
Mijiki	Yuköra—on the Nile
Jungwa	

(ii) *Clans of the secondary Bora splitting*—offshoots of the clans in list (i)

Name of old clan from which new clan originated	Name of new clan	Remarks
Boreŋ	Jokari	The division occurred because the son of the chief of Boreŋ died, and his younger brother, being unaware of this, beat the drum and the people danced. This led to bad feeling, and the younger brother, Kila Jumbe, moved away with his people. Many died 'on the way'. The remainder divided out as follows: Two sons of Kila Jumbe, Wuralek and Kulaŋ,

Name of old clan from which new clan originated	*Name of new clan*	*Remarks*
Boreŋ (*cont.*)	Jokari (*cont.*)	came and settled near Lekulya and Lorogak, who gave them land to the north of the Uguluma road. These became Jokari. Later Wuralek's two sons moved on to live with Bura of Mokido, near Tali. These are Jöri.
	Jöri	
	Yari	Another segment went as retainers to Dari 'because of a quarrel over a woman'. Originally they were named Jungabora. Other Jungabora still live with Jokari.
	Bunja	Resulted from another split in Boreŋ chiefly house. Mar Kulaŋ and his brother quarrelled over rain-power; the elder stayed in Boreŋ as chief, the younger, Dirushuk, came with his rain-making implements, the horn of a dog and a *raga*,[1] to Uguluma, and settled near the small Bora segments of Lomore and Majore.
Jarra	Majore	This separation resulted from a quarrel over rain-power. A stranger came from the bush, divided a small fruit, removed the seeds, and in one half caught the new rain from the sky. He fed this to the Jarra breeding bull. A drought followed immediately. Consultation with a number of seers revealed that the bull had swallowed the rain and had to be slaughtered to release it. This was done and rain fell. The Mar of Jarra then quarrelled with his brother, the founder of Majore, whom he accused of having given the rain to the bull, not knowing that the stranger had done so.
		At this time the Mandari began to disperse owing to the unsettled state of the country. The founder of Majore and the Mar of Jarra went in different directions because of their quarrel. Jarra remained at Kösipi, and Majore

[1] *Raga*, a rain-stone.

Name of old clan from which new clan originated	Name of new clan	Remarks
Jarra (cont.)	Majore (cont.)	went west of Tali to Ginyiki. After a time they moved on to Ajop, 'the place of black earth'.
	Lomore	See p. 23.
Somariŋ (at Tindalu)	Somariŋ (Tali)	This division represents further quarrels in a chiefly line between two brothers. Mar Aku of Somariŋ told his sons to separate. Mar Renjok, founder of Somariŋ Tali, went off with his brother Mar Göbön. On the way Mar Göbön settled with the Bora clan of Mijiki and his people became 'owners of the forest'. This is Togole lineage. Mar Renjok with all his people went farther, to Mina, where they found Nyarkiteŋ, who had previously separated from Boreŋ because of the loss of a rain spear. Renjok was given land and settled. These people are Somariŋ Tali. The two Somariŋ segments still do not intermarry, and would attend the mortuary ceremonies of each other's chiefs. They no longer give cattle on the marriage of daughters. I was told that when the present elders have died intermarriage may take place.
	Tibari ⎱ Ronkak ⎰ Lokweni	Three small lineages living with Tsera near Terekeka on the Nile. Separated to search for new grazing.

With the exception of Jokari, these secondary Bora segments only own a single village or hamlet. Majore, Lomore, and Bunja say they had separate chiefs, prior to government amalgamation. Some of the others have as few as twenty living males; most of them live in a part of the country heavily infiltrated by outsiders.

VIII. *Affiliated Populations of Chiefdoms*

Although chiefly office follows one line of a landowning clan, all clan members living within a chiefdom look on themselves as being of chiefly descent and landowning, in comparison with those other persons who only have residential rights.

The political relations between chiefdoms were always largely the expression of rivalry between owning clans, although the relations between groups of affiliated people had a bearing on the political scene. When chiefdoms were of roughly equal strength competition was expressed in raiding for cattle and in the ability to lead retaliatory fights to avenge death or exact compensation for wrongs. But hostilities were always, according to the Mandari, regulated in the interest of vital, and mutual, pastoral activities. Co-operation was very important; and each chiefdom had to keep its political independence while being, to some extent, economically dependent on its neighbours.

The smaller ones made temporary alliances among themselves, and extensive intermarriage made their interests mutual. Larger ones, though able to stand alone, continually tried to increase their numbers by absorbing remnants of smaller ones broken up by famine, epidemics, and fighting. Traditionally, people deprived of protection and kin looked to patrons of stronger lines to provide them. Chiefs and their close kin were expected to attract potential new subjects in this way. The affiliation of dependents has meant that the populations of chiefdoms are mixed, though this fact is not directly apparent in daily life. Ultimately many members of the chiefdom will have different marriage prohibitions and will perform separate religious rites from others. The exact status of every individual is known, but some status are more readily acknowledged by the possessor than are others. A client will often use the words 'true brother' to refer to an affiliation link and conceal the original client relationship. The word 'brother' does, in fact, reflect the 'brother' relationship of the founder of the affiliated line with an individual landowning protector. Landowners may also conceal non-owning status out of politeness to persons of long affiliation. There is not the same sensitivity about other kinds of non-landowning residence.

The following are types of attachment to dominant lines:

(i) *Client lineages*

Client families and lineages are attached to a protector in a chiefdom other than their own. They perform special duties and cannot move away. They are normally affiliated to a chief or the head of a collateral landowning lineage.

(ii) Settler lineages

These are descendants of larger migrating groups whose allegiance is purely political and does not involve client duties. Many were economically independent (they speak of having brought their own cattle) and were welcomed because of the additional support they could give where defence, entertainment, and raiding were concerned. They were given land to cultivate and are referred to as 'people of so and so', or, when absorbed by marriage, as 'sisters' sons', and 'mothers' brothers'. But their original status of affiliation, that of 'outsiders', is remembered as part of the chiefdom's history. Large settler lineages are potentially dangerous because they can usurp political power.

It may be impossible for the observer to detect whether a line stems from a settler or a client founder, since, over the generations, clients cease to perform client duties, and then, while it is known that they are non-landowners, their particular status may be forgotten.

(iii) Lineages related through marriage

Extended families of relatives through marriage living in a chiefdom other than their own have not, as have owners, settlers, and clients, roots in the country; and permanent residence away from one's own country, if one is a landowner, is rare, and usually only follows expulsion. Temporary residence with in-laws or mothers' brothers is common, but may not produce named lineages. People living with non-agnatic relatives often in fact live in their own chiefdom, because the mixed population permits of intermarriage.

Lineages also originate from children begotten by men outside the agnatic line. In Dari chiefdom, for example, Mar Dara of Dari married a girl with a son by another man. This boy was reared with Mar Dara's own children and his descendants are now Mandiye. Mar Dara paid marriage-cattle for the boy's mother, but Mandiye are not agnates. Mar Dara's own children by this woman form the smaller Kaŋi line, and when giving the lineages of their clan, Dari do not include Mandiye.

The inheriting of wives of deceased agnates, clients, or mothers' brothers produces children who become members of the deceased husband's clan. They are, however, usually marked off from his other children, especially if they live in the village of the inheritor and this is not the husband's village. Bukö and Jamiŋa lineages of Mokido stem from Mar Desa's mother's brothers' wives, whom he inherited. In Bari Kujutat, Deŋa Tome, who was himself the non-landowner founder of Mayar lineage, an offshoot of an early line of this name at Tindalu and now attached to Bari Kujutat, inherited the widow of another client and founded Lörikö line from her offspring. He also perpetuated Gölöri line by engendering children by the widow of the last male member of Gölöri.

(iv) Lineages of dispossessed landowners

Former landowners, as I have shown, were often swamped by others, or merged voluntarily with dominant neighbours. They are found in many chiefdoms.

The structure of attached lineages

Client lineages are inevitably shallow in generation depth and small in population. They are fitted into the owning-clan structure by attachment to protectors who were usually founders of land-owning lineages, and none is recorded as having been attached to an agnate of the undivided clan stem although early clan founders are spoken of as having had clients. Client lines vary in genealogical depth from four to six generations, whereas the landowner lineages to which they are attached have a depth of from five to seven generations. Client groups have shorter lines than their hosts because clients marry later and seldom have more than one wife. In some client lines there are only about six living males. Owing to their small size client lines can easily die out and many are said to have done so during the dispersals of the last century which impoverished their patrons. The names of these defunct lines are remembered.

Client lineages do not have named segments but if they are of long standing, they divide into extended families. Branching off later than the point of segmentation in the patron's lineage is rare, unless the latter is very long. Clients affiliated after this are treated as individuals, and if they are mentioned, it is as 'brothers' or 'people'. The naming of their groups starts at a depth of about four generations. (See Fig. 8.)

Settler lineages approximate to small clans in having larger numbers and sometimes named segments. Some of them also have their own clients. Dispossessed landowners who occupy an indeterminate position, being original landowners but in a dependent relationship with the present new 'landowners', may have a generation depth of eight to ten generations. If there is an original stem and branches of it, the latter will consist of only a few persons. Thus Wejur clan has only three extended families, but they can recite ten generations

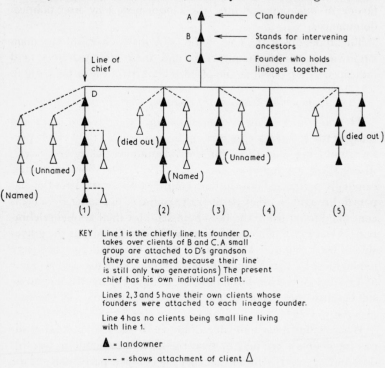

FIG. 8. Typical landowning clan with attached client lineages.

of named ancestors. Jabour clan, the descendants of their early client, Dimu, affiliated to their Mar Rabakak, has six lineages, some of which, individually, equal in number the total population of Wejur.

The attached lineages of a chiefdom vary from one or two to a number greater than that of the lineages of the landowning clan. Dari have six landowning lineages and twelve attached ones, but even so the landowners have a huge numerical superiority. Jungwa, on the other hand, claimed to have no named affiliated lineages but admitted having a mixed population.

The total strength of affiliated lineages sometimes equals that of a small owning line which none the less remains dominant because the former are unrelated to each other and lack co-ordination. Allegiance to the chief will be their only mutually cohesive attribute. Where, however, the numerical balance is overwhelmingly in favour of one outsider line, the landowners may lose political dominance.

The appendix at the end of the book gives charts of the main landowning and dominant clans and their affiliated lines, and indicates, where possible, the place or country of the latter's origin.

IX. *Landowning Clans in the Contemporary Political Scene*

The authentic forms of landownership are those of Bora and those of the few remaining early indigenous clans. Bora chiefs perform rain rites, and those for shea plantations, lakes, and rivers, where these are found in their territories.[1] The Bora rain rites, originally performed only in Bora country itself, were, after the dispersal, brought to other parts of the country, but some Bora clans continued to return to the Bora homeland for their annual celebration. Somariŋ (Tindalu) and Mandari Bora still unite at the graveside of their founder, Mar Desa. Up till a few years ago they were joined there by Bari Kujutat. Other Bora talk of being able 'to come and receive rain' from Bora, but they do not, apparently, go and do so, because they have their own hereditary powers or use rain experts.

When indigenous but later dominated clans have valid landowning claims there may be dual rights in one chiefdom, but this does not necessarily mean that there is conflict, particularly if the over-lords are of Bora stock. The history of each title is known and both groups may co-operate in land ritual. An elder of the smaller group will carry out the ceremony or assist in it and the Bora chief will provide the sacrificial animal.

Early non-Bora landowners have little political power now and such influence as they had, even before the administration gave its support to incoming groups such as Jabour, Mokido, and Dari, was largely religious. Some of them admit to having been absorbed

---

[1] Rain powers are explained with reference to the miracle-working founders —manipulators of rain and water—who recur in the myth. Some of them received special implements—Wöji of Boreŋ got the rain-spear of Mar Nykwac, others had 'horns of dogs' and rain-stones which were used in historical times in Bora rites, but are now said to have been 'lost'.

PLATE II

a. Daughters of a Dari Chief, married to prominent
Aliab Dinka

b. Children with young ox

politically early on. Infiltration and settlement by other people was gradual and brought about by friendship pacts, the handing over of land, mutual aid in defence, co-operation in economic activities, and intermarriage. There was no initial conquest, either by the dispersing Bora segments or by expatriate groups, a fact confirmed by indigenous landowners.[1]

Non-indigenous leaders often have political power now because the external government conferred it on the groups that made the best administrative units. Before the new organization it was possible for small landowners like Wejur, under their own chiefs, to retain their spheres of influence alongside surrounding incomers, the relations of the leaders of both groups being cordial and complementary.

The setting up of the administrative areas upset this compromise which respected the individual needs and rights of the different groups; but it is difficult to see how government could otherwise have been carried out in view of the shift in political power from the small landowners to the more powerful, newer, outsiders. Where true landowning clans were powerful, as for instance certain of the Bora ones, they received government recognition.

It was suggested to me on two occasions that persons of low status received administrative chiefships through misunderstanding, because after the Turkish and Arab occupations the Mandari, being suspicious of administrators trying to discover the indigenous leaders, put forward names of clients or outsiders in order to conceal the identity of true office-holders and thereby protect them from reprisals or unpleasant tasks. When it became clear that this had been an unnecessary manœuvre, the chiefships had already been bestowed on other people.

At the death of an administrative chief, hidden grievances about succession may be voiced, or attempts made to resurrect claims long in abeyance. On the death of Dud Mula of Jabour, Mijiki (under Jabour administrative chiefship) put forward a candidate for chiefly office on the grounds that his was the chiefship by historic right. He did not, however, receive immediate backing, and Jabour retained the chiefship. Lorogok and Wejur would also be justified

---

[1] This is in contrast to Nile history. There small lineages calling themselves *monyekak* were harried almost to extinction by the warlike Köbora from Lafon Hill, who spread over both banks of the Nile. This struggle for land is related to the limited amount available for settlement on the Nile banks.

in putting forward candidates for the combined chiefship but their small numbers would make such action unrealistic. A parallel can be drawn between the alienation of power by numerically strong incoming groups from small indigenous landowning clans, and the way in which a large junior lineage within a single clan may take over the chiefship from a senior but numerically weaker line. This is yet another illustration of the way in which numerical superiority is the basis of political power.

VI

CHIEFSHIP (*TOMATATAN*)

1. *Succession*

EACH chiefdom was under a landowning chief (*Mar*). Mandari see *Mar* as an office in which a number of duties, religious, political, judicial, and social, are combined. But it is more than this, since it denotes a special kind of person, both by reason of heredity and by personal preparation for office. A man must 'be Mar' as well as fulfilling the duties of one. Administrative chiefs, some of whom are the direct descendants of former religious ones, and who may carry out religious as well as administrative duties, are not looked upon as being the same kind of people as their predecessors who passed through installation ceremonies. These ceremonies, which conferred upon them the full powers of office, have now been discontinued, since chiefs can be administratively chosen and rule over non-indigenous divisions.

The Mandari say that before the amalgamations some chiefs, notably those of Dari, who had acquired chiefdoms but were not descendants of true Mandari landowners, went through installation ceremonies similar to those undergone by landowning chiefs. Others who did not do so were described as 'chiefs through their own power, who were not put there by God'.

A chief's traditional titles were, 'chief of the country' (*Mar lo jur* or *Mar lo Baŋ*), and 'chief of the meeting shade and council' (*Mar lo toket*). The word *Mar* can also be used as a mode of address to influential but non-chiefly personages, and descriptively of people who are generous and open-handed (those whose behaviour is chiefly). Religious personalities may also be called *Mar*, the titles of the performers of rain rites and those for shea trees and rivers being *Mar* of such and such natural phenomena. These individuals, while often being so, are not necessarily chiefs.

Chiefship is hereditary in the male line. Eligible candidates used to be selected on grounds of seniority and suitability. Administrative approval is now, also, necessary. In the past a brother often succeeded to office before a son. Much depended on the age of a chief at his death; an old one would tend to be followed by an adult son, a young one by a brother. Then any sons followed after their paternal uncle.

Succession was also affected by the existence of suitable sons of male siblings of the chief, although successors in the direct line were preferred. Only special circumstances would cause the succession to pass out of the direct line.

The Mandari say 'the chief is known beforehand', implying that the office is properly filled by the person who, through his actions and personality, has been observed to possess chiefly qualities. An obvious successor, in terms of seniority, may lack these qualities or not wish to take on the office. This situation was described in the following way:

There may be one son of the chief who is intelligent, who knows how to speak and persuade peacefully, whom the people like to follow. He is generous, always dispensing food to visitors, relatives, and the poor. He is loved by all, because he is *mar* (has 'Mar-like' qualities). The eldest son may not care for any of these things. Instead of staying in the meeting-place to listen when cases are being judged by the elders and chief, he prefers to spend his time in the cattle-camps or hunting with the young men. He lacks a sense of responsibility, and neglects the well-being of the people.

This description of a situation that has been known to have occurred indicates that seniority is not a decisive factor in the choice of a chief. Eldest sons, are, however, in an advantageous position with regard to obtaining chiefships, since they have the first call on marriage-cattle, and their brides are usually the daughters or sisters of other chiefs; they are in a position to make subsequent additional marriages which help them to entertain lavishly and have large bands of retainers. Moreover, they usually represent the ruling chief in his absence.

An example of the successional elasticity which ensured that a suitable candidate for office would be available if there was no heir in the direct line is found in the history of Dari. Mar Aloŋ of Dakotiaŋ, formerly the chiefly lineage, and his eldest son were killed fighting the Dinka. Previously Mar Aloŋ is said to have been inordinately fond of hunting and the life of the cattle-camp, with the result that he neglected his duties. When he was away his brother, Mar Dara, automatically took his place and later succeeded him. Mar Aloŋ's eldest son had died at the same time as himself and his remaining sons were either too young or unable to rally enough popular support. At Dara's death the chiefship passed to his own son by a junior wife, Mar Desa. In the next generation the descendants of Mar Desa's son, Mar Are, had become a powerful group and with the support of the new Sudan administration retained the chiefship. Dakotiaŋ lineage descended from Aloŋ has not held the

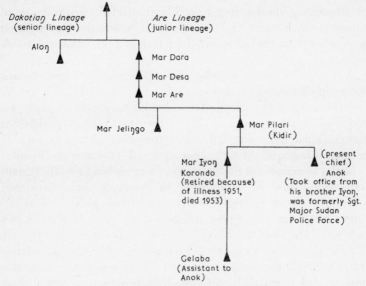

FIG. 9. Chiefs of Are lineage of Dari.

office for seven generations and would be unlikely to get it back unless some disaster overtook Baŋ lo Are.

In default of an available candidate in the senior line a successor from a collateral landowning lineage is eligible. The Mandari say that someone with the right birth and personal qualifications will always be found 'because God will arrange this'.[1]

Hereditary rights of succession had to be backed up by the ability of the office-holder to prove his suitability by gaining a

[1] The way in which chiefship has been spread in any particular clan can be roughly assessed by reference to its genealogy. The prefix *Mar* to a person's name almost invariably indicates that office was held at some point. On the other hand it is not always obvious that a man has held office on account of the habit of using birth-names in preference to chiefly names. Thus Mar Menjour le Payar of Mijiki is generally referred to as Jorji.

reputation for strength and generosity. Chiefship was never held by autocratic power, but rested on the interaction of the two mutually beneficial sets of obligations, those of chief to people and people to chief.

It is said that when once installed a chief could not be removed because a new installation ceremony could not take place during his lifetime. However, should powerful relatives and subjects become dissatisfied with him, they could manifest their displeasure by boycotting the meeting-tree. This indicated universal loss of support, which might lead to a change of behaviour. Disillusioned groups could, in the last resort, if led by a powerful kinsman, break away.

A good chief for the Mandari was a strong chief; a bad one was not a repressive one, though harshness was regrettable, but a weak one. They say with a shrug of the shoulders, 'suppose a chief is a bad man, what can one do? He is the chief.' The individual is distinguished from the office and the office demands support because it is bound up with the interests of the whole chiefdom.

In the assessment of the character of a candidate for office certain traits were held to be undesirable; these were political weakness; meanness, shown by neglect of poor relatives, widows, or destitutes; stinginess with regard to hospitality; quarrelsomeness and rudeness. The desirable chiefly character traits were the opposite of these, namely, political strength, generosity, firmness and restraint, ability to handle people by persuasion and to give wise council. Rudeness is still particularly disliked, and people who assert their authority by shouting and abuse are despised as boorish and ill-bred. The Mandari claim that, ultimately, power lies in the hands of the people themselves. 'He is our chief, we put him there so that he can talk [arbitrate] and we can eat [partake of his hospitality].' They remain quick to criticize the government-sponsored chiefs if they think they are failing in their duties.

The reputations of chiefs were always widely known, and dispossessed persons would try to attach themselves to those with a powerful following, while opportunities were made to leave those whose position was weakening. 'He is no longer chief; a man without people cannot be so. In time someone will come and take his cattle and possessions.' In general, however, the decline of chiefly houses seems to have been due to a series of catastrophes, the upheavals of the last century, famine and fighting, rather than the failure of leadership. Crises of this sort gave other ambitious people the opportunity to step in.

The principal duties of chiefship were the defence of the country, the settlement of disputes within it, and assistance given in the avenging of wrongs done to one of its members by people from other chiefdoms. In order to fulfil these demands it was essential to have a large number of supporters, a state of affairs which resulted naturally if a chief was a member of an important lineage of a dominant landowning clan. These supporters would be reinforced by non-related lines of clients and settlers. Chiefs' villages today still have the traditional settlement pattern. In the centre of each will be found some of the chief's families, those of some of his brothers and of paternal uncles, each with their families of clients. Thus there may be twenty or thirty homesteads dotted around that of the senior wife, where the chief spends much of his time and which is near the meeting-tree. The members of these families will have the strongest feelings of loyalty towards, and single-minded interest in preserving, his well-being. For example, in Dari village, which is rather larger than most, this pattern of clustering round the chief is very clearly discerned. In the main part of the settled area 108 homesteads are spread around the central, chiefly hamlet. The orientation of the hamlets is as follows:

Dari, in the centre with the chief's homestead and meeting-tree.

Rok, about one and a half miles away.

Monshuka, almost adjacent.

Atiŋ, half a mile away.

Asinkwas, half a mile away.

Roto, half a mile away.

A rough count of the people living in this group of hamlets gave 392 souls, of whom 74 were homestead owners, 104 wives, widows, or mothers, 77 were boys under ten. 67 girls under ten, 33 un-married males over ten, and 37 unmarried girls. Of the 392 people, 147 are members of Are, the chief's lineage; 145 are attached as clients of Are or are relatives; 96 are members of part of Mandiiye lineage, related to Are through a female link and their retainers and kin; and 4 are of Dakotiaŋ lineage of Dari. This count is approximate because when people are away for a long time, for instance the youths in the distant camps, people may tend to forget to add them in.

It can be seen that Are form the biggest block, and with the addition of their 145 attached persons far outnumber Mandiye, who are relatives through a female link. Further, neither all Are nor all Mandiye live in these hamlets, and there are other outlying ones belonging to both, which are not included in this survey.

The homestead of the chief's senior wife and its fields are centrally placed. The goat-kraal of his lineage, which is used by close kinsmen and retainers, is near it. All border the dance-ground and the meeting-tree. The Mandari say that the chief must never be isolated, and formerly the young unmarried men always slept in the goat-kraal, and they may still do so when not away visiting girls' courting-huts.

The outlying villages of heads of collateral Dari lineages have the same pattern, and are centred round small dance-grounds and minor meeting-trees.

11. *Economic Obligations*

'*The hand of the chief*' (Kö'yn lo mar)

Generosity is highly respected among the Mandari and there are sanctions that are applicable to the mean, greedy, and parsimonious. A greedy man may figure in satirical songs, or be teased or spurned in the girls' courting-huts. It is believed that the grumbling and annoyance mean people arouse will make them ill. Unsociable behaviour in prominent elders, such as habitually eating at home instead of sharing their food in the hamlet kraal, evokes criticism, which is again harmful (because 'God hears what men say, and assesses people's deeds'). The importance of sharing is emphasized in Mandari upbringing and the young learn to be generous by constantly exchanging pipes, necklaces, or bracelets, and passing on to others anything that is not immediately needed.[1]

Since generosity and sociability is the norm of daily life, a man in a high social position is expected to entertain lavishly. Economic assistance, described as 'the hand of the *mar*', and signifying

---

[1] Chiefs to whom I gave tobacco when they visited me, immediately divided it among hangers-on and others present. This is accepted behaviour and explained by the phrase 'one is a chief'. It may mean that little tobacco remains for the recipient. The non-Mandari provider is made to realize that he must always cater for the indiscriminate crowd who gather round a chief as well as for the chief himself. If the gift is insufficient for a reasonable distribution, everyone present is shamed.

continual giving, used to be vital to the life of a community when there were fewer means of support than there are today, and no administrative relief available in famine. Though there is still need, generosity is mainly important nowadays as a means of establishing prestige. Social values have not yet caught up with the rapidly changing economic situation and this has made it difficult for chiefs to meet their traditional obligations where it is still necessary for them to do so.

Very important duties, now modified but remaining to some extent, were, firstly, the giving generously of food and possessions, and, secondly, acting as a surety against bad times. Help was and still is given in the form of cooked foods, meat, and beer, the distribution being determined by the various types of obligation the chief has to meet. The entertaining of visitors passing through the country, especially representatives of other chiefdoms and non-agnatic kin, also continues. A traveller without other contacts can count on accommodation and food at the homestead of the chief's senior wife. Dinka, claiming in-law ties, now expect to be thus provided for and are a heavy burden in times of scarcity.

When destitution was widespread the chief also made provision for strangers and subjects who had fallen on bad times. In theory, a plea for help should never be refused or a fugitive turned away. Now poor Dinka continue to be affiliated, although few Mandari become retainers. Chiefs were always available to their own people, but the granting of requests depended on how they were placed. A supplicant who was refused, waited for a suitable period of time to pass before renewing his request. A chief was expected to grant requests, but restraint was also expected on the part of the supplicant. 'A man goes on one occasion to beg' (ŋutu wöro mo'yu toparan na geleŋ). Once a request is made it is noted and if possible eventually acceded to. That many claims are made on chiefs is understood and attributions of meanness are only made where refusals are persistent or unjustified.

An obligation was always incurred by the asker, and a chief remembered those who approached him. A man who had been assisted was morally obliged to make a return as binding as the chief's obligation initially to help; repayments were not demanded but made when the debtor was able to do so. Thus in times of scarcity a man could bring his children to the chief's cattle-fire, where they lived on milk, and later, when one of his daughters married, he gave an animal of the bride-wealth to the chief in return.

Small services were performed in exchange for food. A man approached a chief working in his field and took his hoe, saying 'Chief sit down and rest.' The man finished hoeing the field and at the end of the day was fed and given tobacco. Whether or not the help was needed was immaterial. The chief was expected to play a recognized part in order that assistance need not be openly asked for, and to avoid being 'shamed' himself.

A chief distributed old and new implements in the days when iron and copper were scarce. Iron ore was brought from Tindalu, Nyangwara, and Dinka, and copper from farther away. Smiths sold implements to chiefs for use by clients at the rate of three hoe-heads for a goat. Other rich people were able to obtain implements, and both sources were tapped by poor relatives or people without patrons, who would beg for old hoes or bits of metal for reshaping. A chief lent weapons such as elephant and buffalo spears. Now the setting up of bush shops where people buy cheap axe-, hoe-, and spear-heads has helped to free people from this sort of dependence on patrons.

The chief finally had to entertain the influential elders, with whose help he 'held the country', at the meeting-tree.

Assistance given was proportionate to the amount of labour a chief could summon. Sources of labour were individual clients of both sexes, members of client lineages of long standing whose ties to their patrons were weaker but who gave help from time to time, and the chief's own polygamous homesteads each of which formed an independent economic unit which set aside surplus for entertainment.

Groups of young men, some related, others not, came and helped to cultivate the chief's fields during the early spring showers. They arrived in parties or individually and worked on the land of each of the chief's wives. The members of the hut then sowed independently. These helpers were fed and were given beer before work began in the morning 'to encourage swiftness and enthusiasm'. The womenfolk of the men who had worked in the spring and had been feasted came to help with harvest. The weeding in between these periods was done by clients and the chief's own wives and families. People living round a chief's hamlet continue to give this help 'because this is the thing to do'.

The chief is even today presented with natural produce at certain times in acknowledgement of the rites he performs for the rain and the land. What is proffered is left to the individual to whom the chief's goodwill is important. After a hunt a portion of the larger game is handed over, not only because the chief's sons and relatives take part (and formerly because he sometimes lent the weapons used), but also because 'animals of the bush belong to the chief', who includes them in the prayers at forest- and rain-rites. Unfavourable comment would follow failure to present the game, because the chief should 'be treated' (*ge momoysa*).

Landowning chiefs, who perform rites for shea trees, still receive baskets of fruit at an annual ceremony where some of the oil of the last season's crop is ceremonially extracted and used in a rite for blessing the shea groves. Every family which has picked fruit brings a basket. Fish of the first catch is given to owners of rivers who perform the river rituals which open the fishing season. These owners are often, but not always, chiefs.

Small gifts—honey, flying ants, ground-nuts, and pumpkins, are constantly offered. Some are in recognition of past services and others are given with a view to 'becoming known to the chief', and imply a wish for his recognition.

All these gifts, which were made more assiduously in the past because of a greater fear of destitution, made it possible for the chief to relieve distress and to entertain in the open-handed way which is expected of a good leader and one about whom people can boast. Now less is received and less given in return.

There were also other exchanges of commodities which were not directly motivated by economic interest, such as competitive gift-giving between chiefs, and special dances brought to honour them by subjects of neighbouring chiefdoms.

Rival chiefs could ask each other for gifts. If one saw an object he liked in another's house, for instance a spear or bow, he assembled his retainers and went and formally asked for it, bringing with him food and tobacco for distribution. The visitors were entertained by the owner of the desired object which was then handed over and taken home. After some time the chief who had given the gift could make a return visit and, in his turn, ask for something of value. Refusal to comply with a request would 'show that one was not chiefly if one cared so much for a thing. News of one's meanness ("fear") would get round and people would laugh.' A chief must be able to part with something with a show of complete indifference. Only certain things featured in this ceremonial exchange, such as fine examples of craftsmanship or artefacts. Livestock and household utensils were never exchanged.

The type of challenge involved in unconcernedly parting with a precious possession is related to the Mandari notion of being 'afraid'. This means to be unwilling or slow to accept a challenge and involves a sense of shame. A person may be described as 'afraid' if he fails to behave as a situation demands or is unwilling to rise to an occasion to the degree that is expected of him—should he, for example, refuse to receive a dance. I was often met with the words 'Are you afraid?'

Although for the Mandari it is of the utmost importance to avoid losing face by being 'afraid', they recognize the weakness of human nature when they say 'an important man may hide things he likes when visitors are expected'. In the same way a mother's brother conceals favourite possessions when expecting a visit from a sister's son who, by custom, may beg for objects in his uncle's home. The fear of ridicule is strongly emphasized by the Mandari as the reason for complying with these demands; 'people would laugh'.

One of the traditional ways by which praising an important man and begging are combined is for young people to bring him an honouring dance. A dance is generally taken to a chief or notable of a chiefdom other than one's own. The dance leader, 'the owner of the drum', is often the son of the chief or an important elder of the other group who assembles the youths and girls of his village. Once the drums are heard in the surrounding villages the people from them hasten to join in. There are recognized reasons for refusing dance parties. Then the visitors leave without being rewarded. For instance, some Atuot from Atir brought a dance to Chief Anok of Dari while I was living in his village. It was refused because the country was in mourning for the death of his niece, a daughter of his predecessor in office. Should a dance be refused for an inadequate reason shame would result.

If a dance is accepted, a price is negotiated and the dancing lasts three or four days and nights. Before leaving, the dancers receive their dues; formerly these were spears and bulls, and now people dance for money and bulls.[1] Honouring dances make it possible for

[1] Legend tells of an early Dari ancestor, Mar Lubukak, and his friend Wöju, who went to Nyangwara to some people called Korgi to dance for a child. They

young people to meet others from far away, while at the same time enhancing the prestige of the receiver.

III. *Arbitration*

Chiefly pronouncements and judgements (kutuk na mar).[1]

Giving judgements was integral to chiefly office. 'We put the chiefs there so that they can talk', and Mandari never forget that they rule by popular consent. The chief was looked upon as more than an arbitrating elder since 'the mouth of the *Mar* is given by God, that is why we heed him'. Right decisions were made by him in virtue of the personality he acquired at the installation ceremony. The judgements of other elders were listened to only by virtue of their age and experience.

Cases which could not be settled informally, within the hamlet, were brought before the chief and the elders at the meeting-tree and judgements were given. The meeting-tree and the assembly of elders with the chief are both still called *toket*.[2] This assembly remains intrinsically an extension of other types of gathering in the shade which run right through Mandari daily life. A homestead owner always tries to site the hut of his senior wife near a good tree in the shade of which he can sit with relatives and visitors during the heat of the day. If the owner is an elder his tree will serve as a gathering place for the people of his hamlet. More important gatherings will assemble under the trees of lineage heads. The trees of chiefs, being the social and territorial centres of chiefdoms have special features connected with them. They are the few remaining large forest trees, conspicuous because of their size and the wide area cleared around them. Some are shea trees. Many have a long history of use as chiefs' meeting-trees; they are of great

---

asked for a youth to whom they took a fancy but his family refused to give him away and offered an ox instead. After four days the party returned to Mandari, but Lubukak waited behind outside the Korgi village. The boy came by and Lubukak took hold of him and they both disappeared into the earth and journeyed to Dari underground. Lubukak belongs to the early miracle-making tradition; his name means 'to come up out of the earth': (*Lubu*) 'come up out of' (*kak*) earth. The descendants of the boy are Korgi lineage of Rokwe of Dari.

[1] *Kutuk*, language, speech, mouth, or pronouncement.

[2] *Toket* is most nearly represented by the word 'meeting-shade'. The word for shade in general such as that of forest trees is *tilimot*. When *toket* is used of the assembled elders it may be translated as 'meeting-shade members'.

age and have wide spreading roots and trunks intertwined with creepers. The shade they cast at certain times of the day may be anything up to forty feet across. They are usually the most sizeable forest tree in the village and the ground around them, which is used for dancing and assemblies, is kept weeded and swept by clients. Nowadays a bush shop is sometimes put up to the side of the dance-ground so that when people gather there they can also buy things they need.

If a chiefly village moves, these trees are never felled, and some have been pointed out to me that were quite overgrown with scrub but were still referred to as the 'meeting-shade of chief so-and-so'.

Meeting-trees provide a place where the men can gather after the early morning cultivation. The Mandari have a word for passing the daylight hours in a place, and they speak of 'going to "day" at the meeting-tree' (*wörö parana toket*). Those whose homes are some distance away gather at the trees of their landowning lineages. The central meeting-tree is the place for talk, either gossip or juridical. People also reshape and make implements there, and it is, in fact, the centre of the life of the community, where men spend their leisure, do odd jobs, hear the news, discuss personalities, and doze.

Shade is vital to the life of the people, and forming groups under shade trees is fundamental to the organization of their daily activities. There are two types of shade, that of the homestead, cast by the hut and balcony and that of the meeting-tree. Each is the centre of a particular type of activity, that of the home and that of the village and chiefdom. Women do not go and sit in the meeting-shade and men do not spend their time hanging around the homesteads. The meeting-tree etiquette is more formal; youth defers to age and everyone defers to the chief. The behaviour of people in their homesteads is informal because the affairs of women and children are personal. Men only spend time in the homesteads if they have special tasks to perform or are not well, but there will always be men at the meeting-tree, from midday until the afternoon shadows lengthen. The chief and elders sit in the centre where the shade is deepest, the young men and the passers-by sit on the outside or under small trees. When beer was circulated at the tree important people in the chiefdom used to gravitate thither and also people in distress who hoped to find there an opportunity of approaching them. Fighters assembled at the meeting-tree before a foray and the sacrifices for success in raiding or punitive expeditions were performed there.

The meeting-tree has, moreover, religious associations. It is thought that in the cool of the morning and the evening, the spiritual and material world draw closer together. These are the hours when the presences of the dead are believed to linger in this spot, and when the spiritual power of The Above is at its strongest there. For this reason people avoid sitting under meeting-trees at these times lest they should suffer minor indispositions.

Many landowning chiefs possess *Ki* (spiritual power of The Above) and this is thought to pervade their places of assembly. Libations of beer may be poured out behind these trees to free those sitting under them from harmful influences, and also to protect the meeting-place from witches and those with the evil eye.

The assembly of elders was not formally constituted. People who took part in its deliberations were, for the most part, those who happened to be 'daying' at the tree. For important cases influential elders who were away could be summoned, or a day would be fixed for their attendance. Cases which involved people of widely separated lineages demanded the presence of a number of elders from more distant parts of the country, while minor local cases could be settled by the chief and his immediate entourage. Time, in Mandari judicial assemblies, is unimportant and days may elapse before an elder, who must attend, is able to do so.

Complaints at the tree were always initiated by individuals, who brought cases for discussion and judgement when the elders were assembled for other matters or merely for beer-drinking. The assembly was not, except in very special cases, a court in which sentences were passed on the community's behalf.[1]

Speakers, and those who made decisions, were influential persons (*ɲutu duɲ*), who were both skilled arbitrators and the heads of landowning lineages and lineages of long-standing client or outside affiliation—people 'who had the power of words and could convince people without fuss'. Others were close relatives of the chief— paternal uncles, brothers, adult sons, and senior retainers, and clients of deceased rulers. These people were and still are a chief's regular advisers. The young, the poor, or those of low social status took no part unless giving evidence. The Mandari say that before the

---

[1] See p. 132: theft and witchcraft.

setting up of the administration, cases in which women had to give
evidence would have been heard in the chief's homestead, where
members of the *toket* assembled for the purpose. Now, however,
older women may sometimes give evidence in the *toket*. Lineage
disputes were settled by lineage elders at the outlying meeting-
trees, together with cases between their clients and retainers, and
only such cases as could not be settled by them would be passed
on to the chief's tree. Large client lines may have their own minor
meeting-trees.

In big chiefdoms landowning lineage heads became very important. They were often addressed as *Mar* as a courtesy title, although
they were not elected office-holders. In Dari, for instance, there
are several powerful, semi-autonomous heads of landowning lineages who are centres of individual spheres of interest, although
all owe allegiance to the Dari chief. There is, therefore, more than
one meeting-tree:

Dari meeting-trees are as follows:

Landowning lineage Are	*Toket* for whole country at Dari village, named
Landowning lineage Dakotiaŋ	Gomiyo by Korgi lineage, who were living there before Are moved in. Shared by these
Landowning lineage Woŋösek	three lineages.
Landowning lineage Rokwe	
Landowning lineage Surukulya	Share another tree to the north of Dari.
Related lineage Mandiye (two hamlets)	Have a tree in Agwadyr under Butis Agworoŋ, but also come to the central one.

Unsettled cases were brought to the central Dari tree where they
could be heard on neutral ground. The allegiance of clients and
outsiders, though in the first place to their patrons was, through
them, to the chief.

IV. *Ritual Duties of Chiefship*

Religious and ritual duties in Mandari are shared between landowning chiefs, who are responsible for the well-being of their
chiefdoms, and the doctors (*'buniton*), who are also diviners and

PLATE III

Young girls

treat sickness, which is, in general, not thought to be due to natural causes.

The chief, who is a landowner (*monyekak*), must regularly foster the country's natural resources, and in this sense he represents the communal in ritual activities as against the doctor, who represents the specific and the individual. The duties of a landowning chief are inherent in his office and are, therefore, unrewarded, while a doctor's activities are both asked for and paid for.

Chiefs conduct the annual rain rites, which in some countries are the only land rites performed, since at them intercession is also made for the shea trees, crops, game animals, and forest products. Every country has rain rites, but rites for other natural resources are performed according to local demand.

Where shea trees are numerous chiefs 'own' them and hold a ceremony at the end of the season to bless them and ensure a good harvest the following year. The chiefs whose countries have large lagoons, sedge swamps, and rivers perform rites for plentiful water and many fish, and also for the protection of people from illness or injury as a result of their fishing. A political chief may, therefore, be at one and the same time chief of rivers and lagoons (*Mar lo tor*) or (*lo kare*), chief of shea (*Mar lo kumuri*), and chief of rain (*Mar lo kudu*). Whether or not a particular man is in a position to fill all these religious roles depends upon the historical status of his clan and its natural resources. Certain Bora chiefdoms are now virtually the only ones in which all these roles are united with political power.

In Mandari Bora and Rume the political chiefs, Chief Aznaba Lakuli and Chief Fulai Nygwere, who are both administrative chiefs and also descended from the Bora ancestor, perform rain and land rites. Aznaba is assisted by Barisho, head of Mandari Bora clan. (Aznaba is actually of Somariŋ clan and lives at Tindalu, but he holds the Mandari Bora administrative chiefship.)

Even before non-landowning immigrants infiltrated into Mandari, the meeting-tree chief and the person who performed the land rites were sometimes different people. The landowning chief remained ultimately responsible but he could delegate his ritual duties to a brother or head of a collateral lineage or even to someone of client origin. For example, in Mijiki, shea trees and forest game belong to Togole, a small Bora offshoot who joined Mijiki as clients. The Togole ancestor, Mareŋo, according to Mijiki, came from the bush and settled with Mar Mujö, founder of Nolija lineage of Mijiki. He was a great buffalo- and elephant-hunter and was much beloved by Mar Mujö, who handed over to him all the ritual duties connected with the forest animals, shea trees, and the Mijiki lagoons. His descendants perform the land rites while Phulö Diyö, of Mijiki clan itself, performs those for rain. Togole themselves have a small family of clients attached to them, and one of its elders, Könyum, is further delegated to collect the shea fruit at the appropriate time and present it to the Togole 'owner'.

The reason for delegating ritual powers is always known by all concerned, and such delegation creates quite a different social situation from that in which outsiders try to take over ritual activities by pushing out the real owners. The latter sort of action is never truly condoned and it may lead to the neglect of the rites. People to whom rites are delegated as a reward or because they possess some special aptitude, are described as *Mar* or *Monye* (owner) of the natural phenomena for which the rites are performed. The office becomes hereditary, and when the annual rites take place elders of the 'owning' group preside, while the chief of the country attends them and often provides the animal for sacrifice.

There may also be decentralization of ritual powers in the larger countries. In Dari, for instance, there are separate owners of the natural resources in the more widely spaced landowning lineages. As Dari spread over their country, stretches of its river and forest were given to lineage heads. Surukulya lineage owns part of Roro lagoon, Rokwe own a pool at its southern end. Other Dari lineages own sections of the river along the eastern flank of their country. Böndöri clan, who have a mother's brother–sister's son relationship with Dari and are early landowners, also have stretches of Roro river. The ownership of shea trees in Dari is likewise divided.

Division of ritual responsibilities indicates that a clan segmented long ago and that its segments are gradually achieving autonomy, a situation that always results from population increase. It is also related to the number of watering places and shea groves in a country and their territorial distribution in relation to that of the villages.

Traditionally, only chiefs performed rain ceremonies. But now in some places rain techniques which are unconnected with chiefly office or land-owning title, are being operated by men and women. Some have been acquired as a result of intermarriage with the

Aliab and Atuot, others through direct possession by a Nilotic Sky Spirit. The number of these minor rain practitioners, especially in the west, is due to the close relations between some Mandari chiefdoms and their Nilotic neighbours.

Rain experts who are not chiefs operate in chiefdoms where the dominant clan do not own the land or where the rain power has been lost. The chief summons them to perform the rites and provides the sacrificial animal. The powers of these people are recognized as being super-human though they, as individuals, have no special status. This places them in a vulnerable position because they may be held responsible should the rain fail. When this happens they can be subjected to ordeals, a situation that could never arise for a landowning chief, who is regarded as the protector of the land and one who to some extent contributes in his person to its fertility. If his rites fail to procure rain then other scapegoats are found.

Inherited rain powers in landowning clans may sometimes pass out of the chiefly lineage to a junior collateral. I do not, however, know of a case where chiefly rain power has been delegated to a client or affiliated line.

v. *The Ceremony of Installation* (Gwita lo Mar)

To the Mandari, the difference between present-day administrative chiefs and true landowning chiefs lies not so much in the newly acquired administrative status as in the fundamental change of personality the now abandoned installation ceremonies formerly brought about. The mystical element that these ceremonies conferred never attaches to purely administrative office. I was able to learn about the former chiefly installation ceremonies from elders who grew up under chiefs who had been properly installed and shall describe them here because of the bearing they have on what the Mandari believed to be the nature of the chief's office.

The final mortuary ceremony for a deceased chief takes place from a year to eighteen months after his death and the installation ceremony of the new chief follows upon it.[1] At the mortuary ceremony animals are killed for the dead man, grave poles are raised, and the widows choose the men who will inherit them. All the kin,

[1] Mortuary rites for chiefs vary only in points of detail and numbers present from those of ordinary people.

maternal and affinal, living in other chiefdoms attend the ceremony and, because chiefs will have made far-reaching polygamous
marriages in each generation, people from all over the country will
gather together at this time. Important landowners, who are not
related, also come to show goodwill and respect.

Everyone who is related to the dead chief is expected to attend
regardless of latent hostilities which may exist between some of the
lineages or clans represented. The Mandari says 'death is momen-
tous and overrides war'. Only those who are observing the bloodshed prohibitions which follow a recent killing stay away since they
are unable to take part in the eating and drinking and it is recognized
that feelings run high at mortuary ceremonies and that fighting is
quite likely to break out.[1] Violence not only disturbs the solem-
nity of the rites but can be the cause of outbreaks of unspecified
sickness.

Between the burial ceremonies and the installation of the new
chief the country was leaderless, and in the hands of the elders of
the meeting-tree, the deceased's powerful kin, and the recognized
successor to the chiefship. Internal fighting was looked upon as
'bad', being not only weakening politically but sinful and damaging
to the country. Struggles for the chiefship at this time were rare
because the successor was already known, having been either
named by the deceased man before his death or being generally
acclaimed.

There was no complete agreement among informants as to the
proper time for an installation ceremony to be held. Some said it
followed on the mortuary rites and others that it took place some
weeks after the mourners had dispersed. In any case the two ceremonies were closely linked. Once the mortuary ceremony was
ended all association with the dead chief ceased. The usual period
of twelve months between the burial and the mortuary ceremony
sometimes had to be extended to permit sufficient grain for food
and beer to accumulate in view of the prolonged and great festivities that followed. Inability to provide sufficient for both ceremonies might mean that the people who came to the second one
would go away dissatisfied leaving 'shame' and hindering the
installation itself since in theory their presence was necessary to its

---

[1] Garaŋ Aputu, last ruling mar of Jungwa, is said by some to have died from
a spear wound received at a mortuary rite. In this case the wounding is said to
have been 'accidental'.

completion. One reason why visitors attended the ceremony was to express their satisfaction at past entertainment, and it was the duty of the new mar to prove to members of neighbouring chiefdoms, as well as to those of his own, that he could carry on this tradition.

A central part in the installation was played by elders of an adjacent chiefdom, usually of one whose people had intermarried with those of the new ruler. For instance, Mar Are of Dari, grandfather of the present chief, was installed with the assistance of elders of Jokari, traditional enemies of Dari (because of past fighting between them), but also linked to them by marriage. These officiating elders always brought an ox for slaughter to the mortuary rites at which they were also entertained. They came to both ceremonies in order to reciprocate the dead chief's hospitality. As an elder expressed it:

People from a nearby chiefdom who have had hospitality at the hands of the old chief, who have been well fed when they visited relatives or attended ceremonies, who have received bulls or goats or gifts of food, tobacco, or hoes, get together and say, 'Chief so-and-so is dead. Did we not always find him great and generous and his son treated us well and is beloved of all the people. Let us go and take oil for his installation.'

Other friendly chiefdoms attended only as guests.

When news reached the candidate's chiefdom that a deputation from another chiefdom was on its way, preparations for the installation ceremony were completed; a milking-cow was selected, oxen earmarked for slaughter, the prepared beer put on to brew and the food cooked.

The ceremony

The leaders of the deputation were formally questioned as to the reason for their visit on arrival, and the leader who might be a brother, an adult son or a paternal uncle of a rival chief or even his personal client, formally replied, 'the chief of your country is dead, and his mortuary rites completed, it is time for the anointing of the chief and to this end we have brought oil.' The offer was then accepted. A ruling chief did not take part in another's installation.

The delegation was entertained in the homestead of the new chief's senior wife where the ceremony took place. They were given an ox to slaughter for meat, and slept the night with maternal kin and in-laws or in the local girls' courting-huts.

The installation took place early the following morning. When the chief-elect saw the elders assembling he went off into the bush to hide, taking his personal client who had been chosen to go through the ceremony with him and thereafter play a special role in relation to the chiefly office. The deputation followed them and persuaded them to return while they, in their turn, put on a show of reluctance to do so. A ceremony of anointing then took place, the central theme of which did not vary in the accounts I was given, although I was unable to get a complete agreement on the roles played in it by the different participants. In one chiefdom I was told that after being brought forward for the ceremony, both the new chief and the client were seated side-by-side on the newly prepared mats of cow-hide. Another client assistant was then seated by the first client. The elders of the deputation were said in this case to bathe the chief in water and then pour milk, from a cow specially milked to provide it, over his head. This was then wiped off by visiting female elders, who used their hands to remove it from the chief's body, while licking it from his forehead and eyelids. Young women who had recently passed through the ceremony at which the goat-skin skirt of marriage is tied round the loins then presented oil brought by the delegation to its leader, who, together with the elders of the chief's own country, used it for the anointing. As each one marked the chief with it he invoked along the following lines: 'May all evil depart from you. May your body be cool. May you hold the country well and look after your people and feed them.'[1]

Other accounts varied in that I was told the members of the deputation only grasped the new chief and brought him to the mat, where they presented him to the people; then it was old senior clients and important female elders of the chief's own country who carried out the ceremonial washing followed by an anointing by elders of the chiefdom.

All accounts agreed that during the bathing and anointing the two clients sat on the mat at the chief's side, and that the one who was to become his shadow personality was bathed in milk. The other, who would become the chief's emissary, and be sent to

[1] Cool is used to describe a person's physical and spiritual health as well as temperature. To be cool (*tato*) is to be tranquil, well disposed, spiritually adjusted, and in good health. Heat (*tomaka*) denotes anger, illness, hatred, mental and spiritual disorientation. If the chief had a hot body it would be serious for him and for the country which can be affected by his anger and his curse.

surrounding villages and chiefdoms on the chief's behalf and also collect food for entertainment, looked on, and was verbally instructed as to his duties, but not altered as a person by being anointed.

When the chief and the senior client had been bathed and anointed the elders took their hands and joined them saying, 'You are brothers, you must stay together.'

The client was told, 'You are also the chief, when the chief is away you must look after the people and entertain.'

VI. *The Five-day Seclusion*

After the ceremony the chief and his client were confined to their homesteads for five days. Female retainers brought them food and they could slip out in the morning and evening to relieve themselves but could not be seen in public during daylight. The people of the country and the visitors danced throughout these five days.

At this point the chief was given a new name '*Mar* so-and-so', chosen by the clan elders. This became his name of office and was used in preference to his birth and ox names. The Mandari say 'the new name is given so that the chief may rejoice and be strong in arbitration and affairs'. As it was often chosen from among the names of former chiefs it helped to perpetuate their memory. On my last visit I learnt that the client was also renamed.

When chief and client emerged from seclusion the crowds had already dispersed. A sheep was slaughtered for the chief in his homestead, and the meat divided, boiled, and eaten by the male and female elders of the landowning lineage. During this rite a senior elder made an invocation for him: 'You, The Above, and You, The Below, and You Oh our Ancestors, let all evil depart from your person. May you be protected and blessed. God help you to rule us well. May you hold the country and feed us; we wait to receive from your hands.'[1]

After eating the meat, those taking part washed their hands and flicked water on the chief, praying under their breath, 'God help you: may you remain cool.' All were then splashed with water by the senior officiator to ensure their safe departure. Afterwards the chief took his place at the meeting-tree and the elders pledged their allegiance.

[1] 'The Above' and 'The Below'—a way of speaking of God which associates him with the total universe.

VII. *Analysis of the Ceremony*

The installation ceremony of a chief was yet another instance of the ambivalent relations between neighbouring chiefdoms. Chiefdoms, although conscious of being exclusive groups, were dependent on the symbolic act of a neighbour for the installation of their chiefs. Without the visiting delegation, it is said, 'there would be no chief'. Installation reflected the interdependence of countries. It also demonstrated the breadth of a chief's obligations. If hospitality was skimped the Mandari say 'people are dissatisfied and leave, then there is no *Mar*'. Grumbling is always liable to be directed at all hosts whatever their status. Visitors who have a right to beer or meat complain to a master of ceremonies if these are insufficient. Goodwill at all levels is fostered by successfully meeting the obligations of entertainment and is killed by meanness.

Installation was divided into two parts: the rite (*gwita*) and the social background of feasting and dancing (*damaya*). Only the visiting delegation were present at the early morning rite. Visitors from farther afield came later in the day to eat and dance when chief and client had retired into seclusion.

The oxen killed during the festivities and the bull given to the anointing delegation, provided meat for the visitors and were not sacrificial offerings. In contrast, the killing of the sheep when the chief emerged from seclusion was a religious rite following an intense personal and religious transformation. Such protective killings are also made for chiefs on other occasions, and are akin, in some ways, to those made for women who are in dangerous states and for other people, such as killers, who are set apart by having undergone disorientating experiences. The offering made at installation was always a sheep, because sheep have 'cool' meat in contrast to goats whose meat is 'hot'. The Above, the spiritual power which often runs in chiefly lines, is a 'cool' spirit through its association with rain and must receive a 'cool' offering.

Milk was used only in the installation ceremony of chiefs, whereas water and oil are commonly used ritual media. The Mandari say, 'milk is used because it is white, white is a good colour like chiefship; dirty and black things are ugly and bad like clientship'. The chief was anointed with milk because it is white and therefore endowed him with spiritual 'whiteness', incorruptibility, firmness, and self-control. Milk is also felt to be beneficial because 'it is food'; 'it is a living thing'. Water, when used for ritual washing, demonstrates physical and spiritual cleansing, but it is a 'dead thing' and cannot impart positive good. When it is used for purification, anointing with cooling protective oil follows.

White is further the symbol of purity and tranquillity. In rain rites two sheep may be sacrificed, one white and the other black or with dark markings. The latter represents the sky dark with rain clouds, the former, not sacrificed in times of scarcity, makes the falling rain 'white and clean' and gentle because breaking rains can be dangerous when accompanied by violent winds and thunder and lightning.

Milk is a 'living' and a life-sustaining substance derived from cattle, and it is significant that a cow in milk is sometimes sacrificed at the grave of a beloved chief, since cows are never normally killed unless barren. The culmination of the installation ceremony was the bathing in milk, 'it is because the chief has been bathed in milk that he is shut in a hut', 'we listen to the chief because he has been bathed' (*gwita*); 'the reason a chief cannot be removed during his lifetime is that two living chiefs cannot be anointed in the same office'. Of the chief and the client it is said 'they are put in the hut because they have been anointed and their bodies are sensitive' (*pötö*). The chief acquired a new potency which could be damaged, along with his new duties and new name.

The Mandari speak of a chief being '*gwita* with milk' and '*gwita* with a new name'. This word *gwita* is used only in connexion with chiefly installation rites. For other changes of state (usually social ones) affecting other people, the word is *laka*. Thus *laka* denotes the tying on of the goat-skin skirt at a girl's marriage and the ceremony by which the husband is eventually assimilated into the wife's family. There are some features common to the chief's installation and the nuptial ceremonies through which the new wife passes, in that the latter goes to hide and is brought out to sit on a mat with her female sponsors. She is also washed and oiled with butter fat. The girl does not retire into seclusion, but formerly she did not sleep with her husband for a month after the ceremony or before others had been performed, but lived with her mother-in-law. She is also called by a different name by her husband's kin. After marriage she is sensitive to influences which are believed to harm her procreative powers, and continues to be so throughout the fertile years of marriage. Likewise, a chief who was responsible for the fruitfulness of the land was in a sensitive state, and in need of protection.

Angry words and arguments addressed to him or taking place in his presence were thought to be dangerous, and to safeguard him from them senior clients controlled the crowds at the meeting-tree. A spear was never pointed at a chief, nor should one be brought into his presence. When, in inconclusive cases, oaths were taken on spears they were taken in the bush. Sensitivity of this sort is not attached to the present administrative chiefs who are not installed. At a combined Dinka–Mandari court held at Tali the Dinka chiefs left the court while an oath taking on a spear took place, but the Mandari chiefs remained apparently unconcerned.

If an installed chief was involved in serious litigation, a sheep was sacrificed on his behalf on completion of the case.

VIII. *Insignia*

The Mandari speak of former chiefs having had insignia of office, none of which remains. These appear to have been necklaces of large blue beads 'bought for a cow'. Chiefs also used carved wooden squatting-seats like those in general use, but that belonging to the chief was never used by other people and was referred to as *raga*. Chiefs formerly held the large drums used for big dances and for summoning people to hear the chief's wishes. Chiefs still have drums, but now these may also be owned by other people.

IX. *Degree of Executive Power exercised by Chiefs*

From what the Mandari say about their chiefs, it would seem that their influence rested largely on individual character and personality, and the degree of affection and respect any one chief inspired in his own people and his standing among rival chiefs. An aura of greatness reaching beyond their countries, still attaches to some ancestral chiefs, others are forgotten except as names in a genealogy. Apart from the compelling force of individual character, power in chiefly office was derived from:

  (*a*) The chief's position as a member of a dominant landowning
       clan, which ideally represented the largest part of a popula-
       tion and whose members stood together by the nature of
       their mutual interests.

(*b*) The support of armed bands of personal retainers.

(*c*) The chief's religious consecration for office, and the rites he performed for the land and rain.

(*d*) His backing by the meeting-tree council dominated by his own relatives.

(*e*) The small size of chiefdoms.

While chiefship was never autocratic, I think it is reasonable to assume that chiefs were able to control and manipulate the activities of the different groups in their countries, provided they continued to receive popular support.

The political control exercised by present-day chiefs is, as I have explained, derived from administrative backing. The bands of retainers still exist but are much reduced, the meeting-tree councils continue, with new powers, and the religious duties of chiefs remain important even though the installation ceremonies have been discontinued.

VII

CLIENTSHIP

1. *General*

ALTHOUGH the institution of clientship has been modified during the years since administration was established, clients still occasionally affiliate themselves to landowners, and old client groups are found in most chiefdoms. Clientship has been affected by two major influences. The first was the administrative view that clientship was allied to slavery and productive of a category of people with diminished social rights. This disapproval of clientship makes the landowner reluctant to admit that clients exist and inhibits clients from admitting their status. I am sure that no action has in fact been taken against a person for having a client, and this Mandari feeling of government disapproval is probably a reaction to a general levelling out of all status. It means that the presence of an individual client only comes to light after one has been living for some time in a community. There is, on the other hand, little secrecy about being a member of an old-established client group.

The more settled conditions of this century and the lessening of the dangers of famine is the second factor which has reduced the need for seeking client affiliation. Hardship, famine, and hunger remain, but are lessened by government assistance. The Mandari give the impression that formerly famine was a common cause of the extinction of small groups and destitution in general. They speak of 'people dying on the Atuot road' as having been a yearly occurrence.[1] Finally, life is now becoming more egalitarian; factors which made clientship attractive both for patrons and clients have ceased to exist. The loosening of ties of dependency upon patrons has automatically reduced their powers and privileges.

The Mandari speak rather regretfully of the changed conditions now; though the times when clientship flourished as an institution

---

[1] This is the way by which Nilotics still come to Mandari when famine ravages their country. I have met Atuot travelling with tobacco which they hope to exchange for food. Often they are disappointed because the Mandari are themselves short of it.

were hard, they were also full of splendour in their eyes. There was no disgrace attached to being the client of a chief and such a position could be both respected and enviable. Now the client's relationship to his patron has changed. His role is a less influential and a more purely subordinate one. The newly affiliated clients of chiefs and important elders are now almost entirely people from neighbouring tribes, especially from the Dinka, rather than, as formerly, from other Mandari clans as well.

The Mandari word for client is *timit* (plural *timisi* or *tumonuk*); the word *kimaksho* (plural *gunkimor*) is also used for clients in old clan songs. The true client is a person who through misfortune has lost his kin group or, because of some misdeed, has been expelled from it. He needs a powerful protector who will take the place of kin and replace his lost or abandoned property.

A client performs certain duties for his host, and in exchange he is assimilated into the latter's kin group. The word client is really only applicable to an individual in the early stages of affiliation, since once he has married a wife who has borne him children, he has a new kin group which includes the kin of his patron. But *timit* also denotes the status of an individual who has exchanged ultimate personal liberty for himself and his descendants—that is, the right to move away if they so wish—for the protection of a powerful group on whom he and his descendants will be dependent, juridically, politically, and economically, for a long time.

The rights of citizenship that are acquired by attachment to the patron's group cannot be relinquished at will; this is the fundamental principle of clientship. Therefore a man who is living, in whatever economic condition, in his own territory, can never be a client. Ideally, as long as he remains at home his richer kin should come to his rescue.

Timit is also used in a more general sense to denote the very poor and the mean in the way that *mar* denotes generosity and influence.

Client groups are, by the nature of clientship, of mixed origin. Their founders are remembered to have come from the Aliab, Atuot, Moru, Fajelu, Tsera, and other tribes as well as from dispossessed Mandari lines. The distances traversed by fugitives from other countries made them typical potential clients in that they had lost not only their nearer kin but also their tribal membership.

Vengeance killings, famines, and epidemics were the usual reasons for people having to become clients. Children were sometimes brought to chiefs by parents from neighbouring tribes or famine-stricken Mandari villages. They were brought up in the chief's homestead, and acquired wives or were given in marriage as members of his family. Payments for the children were made in grain and the parents relinquished all rights over them. The founder of Akur lineage, living with Bunja clan, was a client of this sort who had been given to Mar Dirushuk by the Moru in exchange for grain and sheep. Juggi lineage, attached to Mundöri clan, are the descendants of a child bought from Tsera by Mar Desa for grain.

There were, however, less honourable methods of acquiring clients. Donodo, founder of Koronda line, attached to Mandya lineage of Bunja, was secretly stolen, as a boy, by Mar Dokolo when on a visit to collect shea fruit. Mar Dokolo was obsessed with a desire for sons and refused to give up the child even when threatened with vengeance. Two other client Bunja lineages are descended from children taken by Lagun Araby, a member of Bunja who is said to have procured slaves for the Arab slave raiders at Amadi. One of these stolen founders was taken from Rume of Bora; he was the founder of Jakari, and two other brothers from Rume founded the other unnamed line.

People who become clients are sometimes said to be those suspected of having the evil eye or of being night-witches. As such they would not have been able to remain in their own country with their own kin, and this is suggested as another reason for their seeking protection. That clients might be witches was a recognized risk patrons took when they accepted them, and likewise there was always the risk that they might later achieve political dominance.

There is a common theme running through the stories that seek to explain the original acquisition of a client, some of which are the accepted way of accounting for an unknown past. This is often 'our ancestor found our client wandering in the bush', or 'spearing leopards in the bush', or 'the wife of our ancestor found our client sitting on a termite mound', or 'by a tree when she was collecting firewood', or 'a child heard a cow lowing and found our client with his ox'. The stories go on to tell how the finder either turned back and spread the news and notables came out and looked, or the stranger was taken back and questioned as to his reasons for being there. He was finally persuaded to settle as a client or asked to be allowed to do so. Some stories specify the country of origin and give reasons for the man's separation from his kin.

Individuals seeking attachment to a new group could also wait at the edge of the meeting-ground until they were approached or the chance of doing some work presented itself, and in this way they indicated that they were open to persuasion. It would be formally assumed that their services were needed as much as they desired protection, an assumption that enables the Mandari to see clientship as initially a free association. It is, despite the obligations it imposes, a dynamic relationship which is modified during a client's lifetime and continues to be further modified for his descendants. The degree to which this happened in any individual case depends mainly on a client's ability to father a large family and acquire property, as well as on the character and position of his patron and the degree to which the client can make himself indispensable.

The following stories show how this dynamic element in the relationship is recognized as an integral part of it. The client concerned in the first tale was a young Bora landowner whose story also explains the foundation of the Böndöri-Nyayo clan.

The founder of Nyayo came from Rume of Bora. One day the mar of Rume saw visitors approaching and ordered his wives to prepare food. The younger, the mother of two boys, refused saying she was tired; the elder at once collected sticks and put water to boil. Later the husband returned and found the youngest also preparing food. He was angry, and asked why she had refused to do so initially (and she had at her side a cauldron of boiling water). As they argued, he lost his temper and threw it over her.

When the girl saw she was disfigured with scalds she lamented; 'what have I to live for, my beauty is destroyed and people will scoff at my scars.' So she threw herself into the fire. Later the husband came back and fearing her relatives took the body and buried it in a hole.

In the evening her son Are looked for his mother. And the senior wife said, 'Your father has killed her because she refused to cook and buried her in a hole.' Then he feared to let his father see his grief, so he made a fire and sat by it with his head in his hands. When his father came and asked him why he was weeping he replied, 'It is only the smoke.' After a while he was hungry and asked the senior wife for food, but she replied, 'Why bother me when I'm busy? Did I kill your mother? Go and ask your father for food. Am I a client that I should wait on you?'

Then the younger brother also came and received the same answer.

Next day Are called his brother and his two dogs, took his spear and bow, and set out into the bush. When villagers asked where they were going, Are replied they were going hunting. They walked all day and the youth followed his brother. He became very tired, and at last questioned Are, 'Tell me, my brother, where are we going? We have already passed footprints of a buffalo far back.' So Are replied, 'Those were only the tracks of one buffalo, we shall find more ahead.' Eventually the youth again questioned his brother saying, 'I am too tired to go farther.' Then Are admitted, 'I have not come after buffalo, but because our mother is dead and we are unwanted. What does it matter if we die? Let us go as far away as we can and look for a new country.'

Eventually, after great privation, they came to the land of Böndöri, near Tali, belonging to a chief with the nickname Penga kwek. As they approached they saw people working in the fields, so they hid in a tree and watched. In the evening the workers went home after hiding their hoes, axes, and calabashes containing seeds under a fallen tree. [During cultivation implements are left on the field, if they are taken home, it signifies that the field has been abandoned.]

After dark the youths released the dogs which had been tied up, took the hoes and began to cultivate. When they had prepared a large piece of ground they slept in a hollow termite mound, putting the dogs on the inside and sleeping across the entrance armed.

Next day when the chief reviewed the work he saw someone had been hoeing. So he called his sons and questioned them, 'My sons, did you return and hoe after we left? Yesterday we only reached this mark, and someone has continued the work.' And they denied having done so. Then on examining the plot they noticed the tracks of dogs. So in the evening when the work was finished the chief stayed and watched. The two boys came out with the dogs, took the calabash of seeds and began to sow.

The chief then challenged them, 'Where do you come from? Are you enemies or friends?' The older replied, 'We are friends, we have now spent several months in the bush, living like animals. Our country is far away; we left it because our father killed our mother and we no longer care if we live or die.' So the chief took them home and fed them. They stayed for a few days, but the eldest was mistrustful and said, 'How can we remain with you? What if our dogs scratch up your fields? You would be angry and drive us away.' But the chief replied, 'Not so; you have helped us and you must remain.' So they stayed with Penga kwek and worked for him as clients. And they were exceedingly strong; if fighting broke out they fought for the chief, at other times they worked in the fields. And the people were very pleased with them. Then after a fall of rain, they found tracks of a buffalo and the elder called the younger and followed after and killed it. He then told his brother, 'Go quickly and tell my master that I am badly wounded and he must send men to carry me home.' So the brother obeyed, saying, 'Send ten men, my brother has been pierced by a buffalo horn.' Then the chief called his

PLATE IV

a. 'Favourite' Ox (*Sönö*)—Nile Köbora (note trained horns)

b. Family in camp-fire circle

retainers and sent them off, himself following behind. When they reached the spot they saw a huge buffalo lying on its side and were afraid. Then Are crawled out from where he was sitting and said, 'Don't be afraid, the buffalo is dead.' Then the people asked, 'What is this, we heard you were wounded and have come to carry you home.' So he replied, 'I am unhurt; this is the thing you must carry home.' Then there was great rejoicing, and they asked how he killed a buffalo with a single spear, and he replied that his dogs had assisted him.

Mar Penga kwek had an exceedingly beautiful daughter, Alak. She never worked like other women, but sat under the veranda in the cool, only coming out to relieve herself. She was exquisitely adorned with beads and bracelets from wrists to elbows. She had rich and powerful suitors, but Böndöri refused them all saying, 'She is chiefly (*mar*)—she must be married to a very strong and powerful man from afar. How can she marry an ordinary person and work like a menial?'

Böndöri then met to decide what could be done to reward Are. Eventually they said, 'Let us give our daughter to Are, so that she can bear us mighty sons.' But Are was afraid. 'How can I marry the daughter of the mar? I have no bride-wealth.' Penga kwek replied, 'This is my wish, and not your affair.' So Alak was given to Are. But he was afraid, and for two months feared to make her his wife. Then an old woman questioned Alak, 'Is all well with you, my child?' And she replied, 'We sleep in the same hut, but apart; all night my husband watches with his weapons at the doorway.' Are then admitted he feared a trick, and that Alak had been given him on a pretext to kill him. Eventually he was convinced however, and Alak bore him sons.

One day a visitor from Rume arrived at Böndöri, and found Are with his family. Returning to Rume he told the father's brother, who was still living, 'Your nephews are alive and serving the Mar of Böndöri.' Then people were sent out to bring the brothers and their children back. But Are armed himself and prepared to fight. Then his master asked him, 'Why are you preparing to fight your kinsmen?' He replied, 'How are they my kin? They have killed my mother;' and he repudiated them.

When the chief of the Rume heard this he did not believe his men, and presumed the boys were held in bondage and his party feared to take them by force. Eventually Penga kwek suggested Rume should pay a ransom for the loss of the two boys and take them back. This was sent, and the younger returned, but Are preferred to remain with Alak and his new kin in Böndöri.

Penga kwek then died, and on his death-bed he called all Böndöri around him saying, 'Now I am dying, and what am I to do? I know you are a very wicked and jealous people, and when I am dead you will abuse my "person" here and his descendants, calling them *timit*. Henceforth Are and his people are no longer to stand as "sister's sons", but as true brothers. To prove this the drum of Böndöri is now to be handed over to them [one of the symbols of chiefship] and if anyone of Böndöri shall speak slightingly of them or call them *timit* they will be accursed and will die.' Then Penga kwek died.

The name of Böndöri was originally 'Nyayo'; then they took the name 'Böndöri' because of their fierceness in battle, leaving the original name 'Nyayo' as the lineage name of the descendants of Are, son of Rume.[1]

This clan is now spoken of as Böndöri-Nyayo, showing the complete equality and integration of the descendants of Penga kwek and Are. The story epitomizes the successful client who sometimes appears in stories of early clients and who becomes a famous warrior, or mighty hunter, or performs some service for his patron, and as a reward is given the patron's daughter, thereby gaining equivalence with the patron's group for his descendants. His true origin is slurred over, or deliberately obliterated. Other points are that the client has to be persuaded to stay in the first place. He, in his turn, tests the affection of his patron by a ruse. The mar loves his client, and follows behind when he hears he is wounded; this mutual affection between client and patron is often stressed.

Part of this story, the killing of a wife with boiling water because she will not cook, is identical with the story of the separation of Boreŋ from Mandari Bora.[2]

From Mandari Bora comes an instance of a hostage client, who eventually founds his own chiefdom:

Sindi, son of Kar Kulaŋ of Bora, went into the bush to hunt. He was away about two months, having gone eastwards and met some of 'the Bari of the North'. [Mandari call the people of Wani Bero, at Terekeka 'Bari']. A fight followed and Sindi was killed.

A seer with second-sight named Yoda told Mar Kulaŋ that Sindi had been slain by the 'Bari of Northwards'. Then there was darkness for four days.

[1] In another version of the story, it is Are and Alak who go back to Rume, after a very large compensation has been paid for them in cattle. The younger brother stays, and marries another Böndöri girl, and it is his people who become Nyayo lineage and are given Böndöri's drum.

[2] In this case, two sons, Wöji, and a brother who goes on and founds Jokari, leave at their mother's death. Wöji takes with him warriors, retainers and cattle, and settles near two small clans, Laŋe and Lokulya. Here, instead of becoming a client, he founds Boreŋ chiefdom. Later, as in the Nyayo story, there is a reconciliation with his father Mar Desa, when he hears the Moru tribe have attacked Bora and taken the cattle. He raises a large army, defeats the Moru, and returns the cattle. As a reward his father gives him the rain spear, Jaliiye, 'for guarding the rain and the land', later lost by Nyartikeŋ clan (see p. 28).

An army was raised against Bari many of whom were killed, and the son of the Mar of Bari was brought back as a hostage to replace the son of Mar Kulaŋ. He was given Sindi's widows to care and provide for.

After a time, the latter, whose name was Amot, begged his master, Mar Kulaŋ, to allow him to return and visit his relatives. He was given three days, but was over-persuaded by his kinsman. Eventually, however, in spite of their persuasions he returned to his master, after a dream in which he learned of plans to kill Mar Kulaŋ. Later on he heard that his relatives were coming to visit Mar Kulaŋ, and knowing by his dream of the plot to kill him, he suggested that Mar Kulaŋ should change places with him. So adorned in fine beads and regalia, Amot sat on the chief's seat and entertained the visitors, among whom were notorious people with the evil eye. The Bari of Northwards, thus bewitched their own son, believing him to be Mar Kulaŋ, who, disguised as a poor client, escaped.

After four days the Bari returned home and Amot fell fatally sick. On his death-bed he called his master and all the Bora elders together and instructed Mar Kulaŋ, saying, 'I have given my life for you, you must now see that my offspring are treated as equals and not as clients.' He then placed a curse on Bora to the effect that if this was not done, death would follow. But the Bora people were unconvinced, explaining that if Sindi, their own son, had not been killed in the first place Amot would not himself have died. Therefore his descendants would have to make their own way.

In time the descendants of Mar Kulaŋ and Amot increased and divided. [In one version Amot's sons begin to contest the Mandari Bora chiefship, in another they have a shooting competition with bows and arrows with Mar Kulaŋ's people, and win.] Amot's descendants by his own wives settled near Tali and became the Bari Kujutat, Mar Kulaŋ's sons, those of Sindi, and those of his widows by Amot, remained with Mandari Bora.

Bari Kujutat, who have the status of an offshoot Bora chiefdom, feel they have true links with Bora. No differentiation is made because of their founder's origin. These people are, in fact, not blood relatives of Mandari Bora at all because all the offspring engendered by, or attributed to, Sindi remained behind in Bora, and only the sons of Amot by his own wives founded the Kujutat. In spite of this Kujutat have remained 'Bora' orientated and until recently returned annually to that country for seasonal rain rites.

Another side to the client situation is shown in the client who steals power from his patron by craft and initiative. This danger, inherent in having clients, is shown in the story of Dimu, client of Wejur clan whose sons gain cattle and wives by a series of tricks, eventually getting the better of their patron himself. In this case the descendants of the client have obtained the chiefship originally held by the patron's clan.

Dimu came from Kic Dinka after having killed his nephew because of the latter's success in hunting buffalo.[1]

Dimu's sister was always lamenting her son, so Dimu left his people [some of whom still live in Dinka] and came to Mandari. He was young and had no wife, so he came and sat under the meeting-tree of Wejur clan. And Mar Rabakak, ancestor of Wejur, asked what he wanted. He then became his client.

After a while, Mar Rabakak gave one of his daughters in marriage to a certain man attached to his clan, who, unknown to the Mar, was a person of the evil eye. The children of this marriage began to die. Rabakak then accused his daughter's husband, who fled with the woman and her children. Dimu followed him, and succeeded in killing him in the bush, and bringing back the woman and two of the children [the latter are later killed because they show characteristics of the father —going out to bewitch people under the pretext of looking for flying ants which swarm after dark]. Rabakak was delighted that the country had been relieved of a dangerous killer, and he gave the widow to Dimu; she bore him five sons and one daughter.

After a visit to Wejur country, Mar Desa, an important chief of Dari, struck up a friendship with Dimu. He visited his homestead and saw his five sons fighting over the teat of one cow; he later remarked the way they were fed by food being put on a flat rock while they gathered round and ate it anyhow. [Their father being a poor client and having only one daughter to bring in cattle, the sons were unable to marry, and had no one to attend to their wants.] So Mar Desa said to Dimu, 'What is this? Why don't you send your sons out to seek cattle for wives? Even if one or two are killed, the rest will remain and marry.' [He implied that they should take cattle by force.] Dimu was angry, thinking Mar Desa was trying to insult him; but the latter reassured him, saying, 'On the contrary, I am right, you are my friend and I will help you by giving you the horn of a dog, and the tail of a rainbow; these will protect you. When you and your sons fight you will be unharmed by spears and arrows.'

So the youths went out to search for cattle, and their owners fled leaving their herds, which the youths brought home with them. Then their sister, Note Duruskuk [which means 'the mother of Durushuk'] made a great complaint against a rich man, saying that he had slept with her. On this trumped-up charge the brothers rounded up his cattle. Finally, Puru, the eldest son, deceived Mar Rabakak, telling him that Tali river had dried out and quantities of fish were stranded in the

[1] On another occasion I was told Dimu came from the Tsera near Terekeka.

shallows; so Rabakak and his men went off to collect them; meanwhile the brothers raided Rabakak's kraals and divided up his cows. On his return Rabakak found the empty kraals and challenged Dimu, who replied, 'I am now an old man and blind. What can I do? My sons, led by Puru, are responsible.' Then Puru went among the herds, and released all the old and decrepit animals and barren cows, and handed them back. Later he also killed an ox of Rabakak's and other animals as an excuse for a valuable bead being broken.

The brothers are then said to have married wives with the looted cattle; each has produced his own lineage which in total form Jabour clan. The descendants of Rabakak have gradually died out. In due course the second brother, Shaka, took the leadership of the clan, 'because Puru only wished to eat and enjoy himself, and eschewed responsibility.' The present Mar of Jabour, Dud Mula, is his direct descendant.[1]

The majority of clients do not succeed in arranging things so happily for their descendants as did the clients in these stories.

However, the obligation of long-established client lines to remain with their hosts is largely a moral one arising from the assistance received in the past and continuing help in need. The relationship evolves into one of mutual interdependence as clients cease to work for former hosts and their duties are taken over by more recently affiliated persons. I have not heard of a client line moving away from their patrons now that they would be free to do so because, as the Mandari explain, their roots are in the host's country. A client wishing to go and live with in-laws would not be prevented from doing so, but for most people it is more advantageous to stay where they are. One client group told me that they moved to in-laws in another part of their chiefdom because they had quarrelled about a pool over which one of their elders had religious ownership. Members of the patron's line, on the other hand, told me that they had been asked to move because they were suspected of having the evil eye.

With increase in numbers and property client families come to occupy a somewhat indeterminate position between landowners and newly affiliated persons. Thus within the client category there is some difference of status as well as a diversity of role.

[1] Lineages of Jabour of Dimu are from the eldest brother Puru, Nyangwara (actually engendered by a Nyangwara doctor who came to treat Puru who was impotent); from the second Shaka, Kawöri; from Jayjuk, Payaya; from Ija, Bari, from Alyörö, Memede (so-called because they were 'always looking', in this case for marriage-cattle).

A newly affiliated client is addressed by name and spoken of as 'our brother' or 'our person' by the patron and his family. He may be *referred* to as *timit* but is never addressed as such unless a deliberate insult is intended. Continuous and direct harping on a man's client status is a recognized form of abuse and if it is accompanied by ill treatment it is considered to be a valid reason for trying to change affiliation. People appear to be sensitive to reference to their status, while accepting willingly the duties it imposes upon them.

Clients are referred to as 'brothers' because this reflects their total incorporation, just as reference to them as 'our persons' reflects their differentiation by blood while implying their residual and other rights. Both forms of address stress the nature of the new client's citizenship.

Politeness demands that non-relatives and outsiders speak of a client as the host's 'brother'. Important clients, formerly chiefs' assistants, were addressed as *Mar* or *Monye baŋ* (head of the homestead)—these are also courtesy titles for a chief's senior relatives. An outsider would never make a direct reference to a client's status, which would be an act of great discourtesy. A landowner pointed out that 'he (the client) is our person. It is not for others to call him *timit*.' Taunting hosts through their clients is a well-known method of insulting. The dance songs which each clan owns often slightingly name non-landowners attached to enemy landowning groups. Such songs are sung during the dancing round graves at mortuary ceremonies which, when they are celebrated for important people, are attended by representatives from all chiefdoms which are linked by marriage. While the songs are being sung, people who are named in them from other chiefdoms sit down in protest. This is yet another instance of the competitive nature of chiefship and personal attachment to particular countries.

The singing of songs directed against non-landowners can lead to fighting. Mokido composed a song against people attached to Dari which caused a fight between the two clans, and a number of people on both sides were still in prison during my visit as a result. Dari are sensitive about the song because Mar Are, grandfather of the present chief, helped Mokido before they became powerful.

I witnessed a scuffle during a dance when an elder who was named in a song threatened the singer with a spear.

The client and his family use the host's clan and lineage name until the group of client descendants has grown sufficiently large

on significant conversations. He is expected to know all the current news and to decide what should be passed on to the chief. He 'has the ear of the chief'. In pre-administration days clients acted as spies for their patrons, eliciting information about cattle concentrations and fighting strength. Such spies, if discovered, were killed, and the fear that dissatisfied retainers would go off and become informers for another chief was given as a reason for their having upon occasion been intercepted and killed.

Clients cultivate their own fields and their crops are used not only for feeding their families but also for the entertainment of neighbours. They are expected to lend a hand if their patrons have visitors, but also get help themselves in return. They are in a position to acquire a herd, since at the marriage of their daughters, the bride-wealth is divided between the father and the patron who has helped to provide the bride-wealth for the girl's mother. If a girl of client family marries a wealthy man, cattle as well as sheep and goats are passed.

Even when the bulk of the bride-wealth paid for a son's wife is provided by the client's kin, an ox is sometimes given to the head of the host's line on the marriage of a daughter, because the host's people are 'kin' and should, therefore, receive the 'ox of brothers'. Individual clients may likewise receive an animal on the marriage of the patron's daughter, although such payments are not made regularly by lineages of hosts to long-standing client lineages.[1] The degree to which payment may or may not be made depends largely on circumstances. The Mandari speak of clients as having formerly few, if any, cattle but many sheep and goats which were the traditional animals for client bride-wealth payments.

Clients normally marry only one wife although the personal attendants of former chiefs are said to have had more, depending on the wealth of the host line and the degree of personal affection felt for the retainer. But it is also quite usual for people who are not clients to marry only once, so that having only one wife does not necessarily differentiate clients from others. It was also the practice for clients belonging to minor client lines to marry women of similar status, although some fathers of non-client daughters were prepared to accept a small bride-wealth if a marriage served to link

[1] On the marriage of the chief's daughter referred to on p. 50, an ox was given to the chief's personal retainer and animals were ear-marked for heads of groups of various affiliations.

their family with that of a client son-in-law's wealthy patron. Girls of client lines are often married by landowners and chiefs as junior wives. (A chief's senior wife should be the daughter, sister, or cousin of a rival chief or of one of his kinsmen, as such marriages form the basis of important political pacts, and these marriages still take place. The daughter of a Mandari chief may also be married to an Atuot or Aliab chief.)

Marriage customs are now freer than formerly and youths of long-standing client lines can marry where they like if sufficient cattle are available. These young men attend dances and girls' courting-huts like their landowning age-mates, and if the girls fall in love with them their fathers may be forced to consent to the marriages regardless of conventions.

An individual client, however, recently attached to a patron, would never have collected sufficient bride-wealth to marry a girl of high standing and the marriages of new clients were, and are still to some extent, arranged by their hosts with fathers who are prepared to agree to them. They were formerly given the daughters of other clients or female hostages; the bride-wealth, if any, being merely a token payment. If a host would not or could not find a wife for a client the latter could, after a period of hard work on his fields, marry for grain.

A patron never marries the daughters of his own clients or of his clients' immediate lineages. Such marriages would be inconsistent with the patron–client relationship. The Mandari stress the fact that two lines linked through a client–patron situation must be kept free from the tensions inherent in affinal relationships. Marriage is, however, permissible between landowners of different collateral lineages and client women attached to each. Marriage prohibitions of this kind affect only true clients and not settlers.

The client marriages described in the story of the Böndöri-Nyayo and that of Dimu, in which a host gives his daughter to a client, are direct breaches of custom as to client marriages. They were made specifically for the purpose of raising the status of the client and his descendants, the patron's daughter is treated as a male and takes the position of a son of the line so that the offspring will be landowners. This is clearly seen in the Böndöri-Nyayo case where the use of both names together implies the equality of the two lineages. These stories also reflect the Mandari awareness of the potentialities of the client status.

Clientship enabled those without kin to achieve varying degrees of importance in groups other than their own. And because Mandari society is essentially egalitarian there was no possibility of a class of clients as such emerging. Within his chiefdom a client would be known, but to the members of other chiefdoms he became one of a group of 'friends', 'enemies', or 'relatives'. Should there be a question of marriage, however, the antecedents of both parties would be inquired into more closely.

Clients have always suffered under certain quasi-legal disabilities. Thus a recently affiliated client could not easily bring any claim against his host or the host's relatives. Now, as the categories of host and client are not recognized in the government courts, a client can bring an action against his host, although this is, I am told, rarely done because the force of customary behaviour of client to host is still strong. Moreover, since the plaintiff is dependent upon the defendant for his livelihood, little is to be gained by such a course of action. One has the impression from present evidence and from what the Mandari say, that the persistent abuse of clients by patrons was rare. Public censure was feared; and the rivalry and friction between kin who are equal in status and have mutual rights in property was never present in the client–host relationship.

Clients bring cases against those who are not their hosts, and the latter will then speak for them and assist them in paying compensation when judgment goes against them. Such 'legal' assistance has always been an obligation for a host. Similarly if a client or his property sustained hurt or damage he was compensated, and, if he was killed, his host was indemnified. Cases concerning clients attached to people from different chiefdoms were formerly settled under the threat of vengeance.

Established client lineages have always had a degree of autonomy in settling their own affairs and paying and receiving compensation. But litigation is complicated if the property of the client and that of the host lineage is in some degree mutually held. Where bride-wealth has originally been received by virtue of a proto-kin relationship with a host line but these payments have been discontinued, a position is reached where members of each line can indemnify the other.

People can bring cases against the clients of their kin and I heard of a case in which the brother of a chief brought a case against the latter's client and received compensation.

Formerly, individual clients or small client families were in some ways in a disadvantageous position *vis-à-vis* their patrons. If the relationship was abused there was little redress and the idea of 'brotherhood' was binding only in certain contexts. On the other hand, many privileges could be enjoyed. Treating a client well was sanctioned by the disgrace attached to maltreating dependants, but undoubtedly neglect of clients did occur. The Mandari attribute it to human failing, unless obviously the result of a change in the circumstances of the patron himself. It is admitted that the client's main weapon if wronged was a change of allegiance, to which he also had recourse if he had wronged his host.

Should a host kill a client the latter's family was not indemnified. The Mandari say 'it is up to the chief, if he kills a client it is his own affair'; but this is said to have happened only in cases involving the evil eye, witchcraft, killing of a host's kinsman, or violation of his women.

Because the client–host relationship was a complementary one devoid of the tensions that develop around cattle and women in true brotherhood, it was important for chiefly families, especially, to have these strategically placed 'client-kin' who were fundamentally uninvolved in kinship and succession rivalries to act as advisers and assistants.

11. *The Role of the Special Client*

The role played by a specially selected client in the installation ceremonies of a chief lay at the heart of the client–host relationship. His duties were more fundamental to the functioning of chiefship than those of ordinary clients described in the last section. The individual concerned was also different from other clients because he was 'by the side of the Mar' while they were 'outside'.

He was chosen by the new chief and the landowning elders, and he might already have served a deceased chief and be installed a second time, or again he could be selected as having displayed outstanding abilities. He was normally younger than the chief, and if a client was too old for reinstallation, a suitably qualified son would replace him. Thus the office tended to be hereditary and lines of chiefs and clients were linked together through several generations.

Once the installation ceremonies were completed and the chief and his client had emerged from seclusion, the client became the shadow personality of the chief. He was 'Mar as well', and in the chief's absence could speak for him. Since an installed chief had to avoid argument and the use of harsh or angry words and did not order people about ['he should speak only good and agreeable words'], the client gave orders and reprimanded people and restrained them from shouting and quarrelling at the meeting-tree. For a chief to be involved in situations in which hostile feelings were revealed, adversely affected his health and spiritual virtue. Former chiefs, though vigorous and powerful leaders, seem to have kept apart to some extent and to have made their wishes known through intermediaries. The client could even sum up a case in the chief's absence: 'He knows what the chief would say and says it for him.'

Certain kinds of intimate behaviour are said to have existed between a chief and his personal client, particularly in their eating habits. Abundant food was cooked in the chief's home-steads and carried to wherever he was eating with his close kin and his advisers. After he had sampled a dish the special client, who sat just behind the chief, leant forward and removed it, wiping the chief's mouth with his hand at the same time, and saying, 'My brother, why do you spoil your palate with filth like this?' He handed other food to the chief, finishing the first lot himself. He could take any food that he fancied in this way. The Mandari joke about the chief being in the hands of his client: 'he is hungry because as soon as he tries to eat the food is taken away.' They say, 'his wife must cook delicacies for him at night when the client is asleep.' How far this feeding custom was really followed it is difficult to say, but it is still talked of.

The client could also help himself freely to the chief's tobacco, or obtain it by saying, 'visitors are here and wish to smoke.' The chief could likewise borrow tobacco from his client.

The client constantly watched over a chief's needs. When travelling he always walked in front of him to remove thorns or creepers and give warning of roots and stumps while others followed to protect him from the rear. A chief was encircled as well by a large body of armed retainers.

Special clients were also peacemakers. 'If a chief quarrelled with his wife his client might take his hand and lead him away.' The client's advice was constantly sought because 'he had the ear of

the chief and knew his wishes.' A prominent client's influence
could be far-reaching; people obeyed his orders and followed his
suggestions.

The institutionalized familiarities permitted between a chief and
his client reflected the closeness of their relationship, which was
made possible by the fact that every element of rivalry had been
eliminated, since a client could never become a chief. The Mandari
see the decline of the roles of chief and of client as linked, and say
'there are now no chiefs because there are no clients.' Clientship
is debased and chiefs are no longer installed. 'They (chiefs) are
owned by the government and not by the people.'

An old Bora myth stresses this close relationship between chief
and client. The client figuring in it is named Lupöyut and the chief
is the mythical Mar Desa.

When Mar Desa died, his client Lupöyut asked to be buried with
him, saying, 'who will feed and care for me now, and see that I am not
abused and who will care for my wife and children?' He climbed down
into the open grave while all the people reasoned with him saying, 'wait,
your time will come, because all men must die.' They pleaded with him
till sunset when they were exhausted and eventually, as he would not
be persuaded, they laid the body of Mar Desa beside him and covered
them both with earth. Lupöyut was heard groaning under the earth for
five days, then there was silence. His spirit became very powerful because
he died by his own hand and was not called by God. In spring, when
rain is needed, Bora people come to sweep the grave of Mar Desa and
Lupöyut bringing beer, grain, shea butter, and oxen. The oxen are
slaughtered on the grave and the beer drunk; then the people dance,
and when they return home rain falls on them on the path.

Lupöyut is shown as choosing physical death rather than
possible social extinction, and fear of being abused after the
death of a patron is a recurring theme in stories of the last requests made by favoured clients.[1]

III. *Analysis of Client Institutions*

Apart from the myths in which clients feature in association
with their patrons, the Mandari throw no light on the origin of
clientship. Various suggestions, however, could be made. For
instance, if the Bora people were initially a group of powerful
incomers from outside Mandari (possibly of Luo-speaking stock),

[1] See the stories of Sindi and the Nyayo client.

it could be assumed that the client–host relationship was the way they absorbed a small scattered population already *in situ*. Surrounding groups and later incomers then adopted clientship as a means of building up their own chiefdoms, which Bora sometimes speak of as being modelled on theirs. Again, it might be that clientship was always common to the Bora, whoever they were, and was merely continued by them on their arrival in Mandari and spread among other inhabitants. Further, clientship could have always been a permanent feature of a society which was divided into landowning lines with religious powers, and non-landowning lines who lacked these powers and played a complementary role.

Among all Bari-speaking tribes types of dependent affiliation are found. In Bari there are several classes of dependant, the most menial, the *'dupi*, may have been different ethnically from their Bari overlords. According to Whitehead the Bari described them as 'shorter and fatter, with reddish skin, spreading noses, broad faces, and small eyes'. Whitehead has the view that the *'dupi* were of a different stock from the Bari, who he believes were a cattle-owning people akin to the Masai and Turkana.[1] The *'dupi* appear from the literature to have had far greater disabilities than the Mandari clients, although many points from Seligman's and Whitehead's accounts bear strong resemblance to what we find in Mandari.[2] The Bari also had a category of war captives and people who affiliated to protectors because of economic necessity, called *pena*. Some of these were of the *'dupi* class. In the causes and effects of their attachment they appear to approximate more to the Mandari clients than the *'dupi* proper, although little is said about their status or role in the society. Where Bari clients appear to differ radically from those of Mandari is that these 'non-free' classes, as Seligman calls them, were directly opposed to a specific class of 'free-men', known as *lui*. No class of 'free-men' as such exists in Mandari.

Father Crazzolara in his accounts of the Luo migrations also gives some interesting details of people like clients.[3] In what was

[1] G. O. Whitehead, 'Social change among the Bari', *Sudan Notes and Records*, vol. xii, 1929, pp. 91–97.

[2] C. G. Seligman, *Pagan Tribes of the Nilotic Sudan*, George Routledge, 1932, chap. vii, The Bari. Also Nalder, op. cit., p. 14, chapter on 'The Bari', by A. C. Beaton.

[3] J. P. Crazzolara, *The Lwoo*, Instituto Missioni Africane, Verona, 1951, part ii, chap. viii, 'Miscellaneous Notes on the Alur'.

Alur country, later overrun by people of Jo-Luo origin, the Jo-Luo
provide the ruling families, while the Alur (composed in turn of
diverse peoples) work for these masters as well as for themselves.
One Alur group, the Okebo, is described as 'the sole craftsmen,
particularly metal workers'. Another category are 'king's slaves';
some of whom were war captives. These had various duties in the
royal house, running errands, and accompanying royal masters on
journeys. An office of 'stump indicator' appears (as with the Mandari), a man who walked in front of the 'king' and warned of
obstructions. He is a special attendant spoken of as 'being rewarded
with a wife after a time of service'. He also performed other
'personal services'. These and other attendants might make free
use of the possessions of the 'king' (*rwot*), and if found doing so
would explain with a show of respect that such and such an object
was no longer fit for the use of the *rwot*. Crazzolara also says 'these
intelligent dependants in time provided themselves with possessions, and prepared little by little the independence of themselves
and their dependants.' Finally, he speaks of boys and girls being
paid in compensation for homicide who became attendants in royal
houses. From what we can glean from his account, the duties and
status of many of these retainers were very close to those of retainers
attached to ruling or wealthy Mandari lines, except that the Mandari client is not necessarily ethnically different.

Mandari client affiliations have a complex pattern, which does
not completely accord with any straightforward solution. Every
kind of affiliation exists. While it is true that certain early inhabitants affiliated themselves to powerful newcomers, or to expanding
groups like Bora, many never became *clients*, because clientship in
Mandari primarily denotes a loss of land and kin, and a lack of
civil rights. Early submerged groups were never destitutes in this
sense, and indeed are still recognized by protectors and brought
forward as the first citizens. They would be indignant, if it were
automatically assumed that they were clients, although in some
cases they may be. Many clients came *into* Mandari from *outside*,
and needed the citizenship which they acquired with their affiliations. The initial type of contact between patron and dependant
then developed in a variety of ways. Some incomers or migrating
peoples were given land by groups previously claiming to be
owners and dominant, but later becoming submerged. There are
also examples of the handing over of landownership and the ritual

PLATE V

Crossing to cattle camp—Nile Köbora

duties relating to it by small established groups to larger incoming ones in exchange of cattle. Some clients were outsiders, some were destitute or fugitive Mandari from rival chiefdoms, some were even from Bora segments. The full evidence does not therefore wholly support Dr. Middleton, when he writes:[1] 'This process of differentiation (client-type affiliations) provides a means of bringing aliens into the society . . . the original settlers perhaps becoming associated with the earth cult, while invaders become associated more with a purely political chiefship.'

There is no clear-cut distinction of this kind in Mandari, although some incomers do now hold political office, having left religious office to superseded patrons.

An important point also is that no client class as such exists drawn from any one population. In one chiefdom an indigenous group will be found as patrons and in another incomers fill this role. Both chiefs and clients may be of either category. Even Bora, whose clans seem to have generally achieved and retained political dominance, have a few split-off segments which are client, not landowning. The fundamental mode of assimilation of one people, group, or individual to another has been successfully adapted to suit a wide variety of historical situations. The Mandari themselves know this.

IV. *The Client Today*

It is no longer easy to distinguish a client from his host's relatives and other settlers. There are now few individually affiliated clients and those there are, are assisted in their work by ordinary people. In the fields they cultivate alongside the host's kin and without intimate knowledge of everybody's relationships it is impossible to tell a client from a landowner. I have met individually affiliated clients, some of whom are young and unmarried, and there are still many people belonging to former client families who give the traditional assistance. In Dari, small client extended families are clustered round the chiefly house. One stems from an Aliab Dinka who came to Mar Are (grandfather of the present chief) during a famine. Another is descended from a Dinka who was the lesser assistant at the installation of Mar Are. Two other small lines stem

[1] Edited by J. Middleton & D. Tait, *Tribes without Rulers*, Routledge & Kegan Paul, 1958, p. 18.

from affiliations to Are. These extended families have from five to twelve adult males. A further line of three generations was founded by a Dinka doctor forceably taken as a hostage to compensate for his seduction of a wife of Mar Desa, father of Mar Are, while she was under him for treatment.

Another family of five persons are descendants of a client of Mar Pilari, father of the present chief of Dari. There is also an important line which provided the senior client assistant installed with Mar Are. One of its elders is the present chief's right-hand man. He is a forceful individual and is the person who will lead the Dari mourning party when it attends mortuary ceremonies in other chiefdoms. He is also a government headman.

The administration has recognized the traditional duties and status of heads of client lines by giving them minor administrative offices within the new political divisions. Clients of lower status can serve their chief as tribal policemen responsible for rounding up offenders or collecting compensation. They carry on the tradition of guarding the chief and his village, carrying out his orders, and keeping the peace. Not all the chief's police are former clients. Many important doctor-diviners, some of whom have accumulated considerable wealth, also come from client backgrounds.

Clients and their kin who are still closely attached to a chief work in the chief's fields as well as in their own. They have a variety of duties to perform in the hamlet and are in evidence at any important event—a big court, the arrival of visitors, public entertainment, the visits of the district commissioner, and so forth. It was a retainer of this sort who kindly helped me in my camp, acting as watchman while I was away visiting other places, and helping to cut and fetch firewood, an arduous task that involves long walks and local knowledge. This man kept me *au fait* with current happenings in the village and gave me much general information about it. No payment was negotiated since he was providing a traditional service; the amount of the reward being determined by the importance of not appearing 'mean'. Some individuals and small groups were still, then, receiving help in court cases and bride-wealth payments and my watchman, who was having difficulties with his in-laws over an outstanding marriage-goat, assured me that the chief, 'who is our father', would supply it.

An old chief from Dari who had retired on account of illness and had been succeeded by his brother, had a personal client named

Maluŋdit who had come from Bor Dinka as a youth. He was still unmarried although, so the chief's daughter told me in 1951, efforts had been made from time to time to find him a wife. He had no cattle, as the animals that had come to him on the marriages of the chief's elder daughters had all died. He had expectations as a result of negotiations that were then going on for the marriage of a younger daughter. He was a very old man, tall and thin, and though food was available for him from the chief's homestead he ate little and was said to chew and smoke tobacco instead. At beer parties he had his own gourd of beer, and drank together with the elders of the line. He was renowned for the energy he displayed in cultivation for one of his years and he would clear huge fields for the wives of the ex-chief and those of his brother, the present office holder. He slept in the goat-kraal on a wooden frame above the dung fires and kept watch over his patron's huge herd of goats. Maluŋdit was described as 'a great man of goats'. His lean figure was always to be seen at the meeting-place where he stood around seeing that all was well. He was held in affectionate esteem and was, undoubtedly, a personality in his own right.

On my return in 1958 I missed him and noticed that the earth was smoothed over where the goat-kraal had formerly stood. I was told that he had died shortly after the death of his master and had been buried under the kraal where he had lived and worked. No grave poles had been set up for him but I was told that this was because of the previous famine years, and that the grave of his patron had only recently been completed.

A client with no kin should, theoretically, have the mortuary rites, including the raising of the grave poles, carried out for him. These are essential to the quiet repose of the dead and if they are neglected the living will fall sick. When a client dies without kin —a patron's kin are not of the same blood—people do not feel so compelled to raise poles, as there is no one left to suffer if it is not done. People tend to perform the rites from affection or as recognition of good work or from fear of public censure.

A Mokido elder has a young client who came to Nykwac of Loriŋa when his own father died in Dinka-land and left him without kin. He lived as a member of the family and Banye, the son of Nykwac, told me that they would shortly find a few animals so that he could marry. From his appearance he looked a little beyond the age when non-clients find a wife. He hoed, cut and fetched wood, and cared for the goats. He appeared to be treated like other sons of the homestead.

There is one unpleasant aspect of the client situation which remains prominent today, and that is the association of night-witchcraft and the possession of the evil eye with non-landowners. I constantly came across client lines which were under this stigma and individuals from them who were thought to be actively engaged in these practices.

That some lineages from among the population of a chiefdom should be thought to have dangerous ritual powers is understand-able when it is remembered that members of dominant landowning lines can always give proof of the purity of their stock by evidence based on known clan history and genealogy, whereas clients are often in no position to do this if they have 'come from the bush'. Not all client lines are, of course, believed to have these traits, and specific ownership of them is related to incidents in the history of a particular line which are connected in peoples' minds with sick-ness, death, and misfortunes of their own kin.

The belief that bad ritual elements may be inherited by those who are not connected with the land by birth is complementary to the belief that landowners have beneficial powers by virtue of their ownership (*komonyekak*).

Witchcraft is thought to arise from many causes, but the most common among the Mandari, as among other African peoples, are poverty, envy, and hatred. Landowners are, ideally if not in fact, rich, powerful, and generous, while clients are poor and politically weak. Therefore, as a type, they are expected to be envious, and if they come from lines of witches or ones having the 'eye' they are believed able to harm.

It is quite usual for persons closely affiliated to a patron to be thought of as harming him or his kin, and this sort of suspicion can lead to eventual expulsion of a client group, and in the past has sometimes led to its extermination. Today, when witchcraft can no longer be made a reason for bringing a person before the meeting-tree, it is used to explain the undiagnosed illness and petty annoyances of everyday life. Although anybody may suffer in this way and a witch may attack anybody, the landowners are felt to be particularly likely targets for these attacks, because they are in a position constantly to arouse jealousy.

The cause of unexplained ills is often expressed in terms of hostility to marginal groups and witches of opponent's countries, thereby pointing up political rivalries. The circumstances surrounding notorious events which are laid at the door of supposed witches are made public by gossip, and more especially by songs which often contain descriptions of dirty and anti-social behaviour and perversions which occasionally occur, and which cause considerable suspicion if the objects of them are of borderline status. The slur of possessing bad ritual powers is one more example of the ambivalent attitude that is taken towards clients.

VIII

SOCIAL CONTROL IN CHIEFDOMS

1. *Force*

IT is extremely difficult to gain an accurate picture of the way in which force was used as a political mechanism in pre-administration days, since all our knowledge is hearsay, though some of the facts that Mandari give can be confirmed by the way they still behave. People may resort to force even though, being illegal, it results in punishment by the legally constituted authorities. Moreover the threat of force is still used, and preparations are made which stop short of actual violence. Situations of this kind arise particularly in connexion with offences against women which arouse violent emotions and offend pride. A woman's kin may arm themselves and make hostile demonstrations against her seducer, refraining, however, from actually killing him. The chief and the elders quickly intervene, calling together people from both sides and trying to arrange an interim settlement in order that peace shall be maintained.

The Mandari say that it was socially accepted in pre-administration days that no compensation was paid for homicide, which always called for retaliatory action. This is in line with a generally stated principle that between agnatic kin (a concept that embraces the total clan) compensation cannot be paid because all are 'brothers', while beyond the clan, disputes involving killing cannot be settled by payment of compensation because the two groups stand as 'enemies' to one another. The Mandari admit there were various kinds of compromise between these two extremes in real situations.

Except within the kinship group, some sort of direct action on the part of an injured person to gain restitution was socially recognized, provided that such action was kept within reasonable bounds and did not disrupt the more important economic and social ties.

The Mandari equated human life with women and not with

cattle. When compensation for homicide was paid from one un-related group to another, one or two female children were handed over. Men were also said to have been given in exchange for a life taken. Cattle were used for compensation payments only where, because there were cognatic or affinal kinship links, men or women could not pass from one group to the other, but the need for pay-ment was recognized.[1] Minor injuries were also compensated with cattle, the number handed over being negotiated in line with a recognized scale for loss of limbs, teeth, &c.

The threat of force could be used in various ways and at two political levels, that of the chiefdom when violence was threatened or used within it, and between chiefdoms.

11. *The Operation of Violence between Chiefdoms*

Between chiefdoms force, or the ability to threaten its effective use, was the ultimate political weapon, and it was often the only way in which wrongs done by one chiefdom to another could be settled.

If a man killed or wounded someone of another country the victim's clan sought vengeance for reasons of prestige and to exact compensation. The killer's kin, recognizing this as the correct reaction, prepared to receive attacks of the victim's kin. The latter would try and kill the homicide himself or an agnate of his age and status. The victims were marked down in advance, but kin and neighbours might also become involved in the fighting.

When the killer and the killed came from chiefdoms which were traditionally hostile because of past wrongs, or their countries were territorially far apart and there were few social ties between their peoples, neither would consider settlement through arbitra-tion. Wrongs were often, in fact, made an excuse for taking cattle and settling old scores, and revenge parties were collected or supported by chiefs and a large number of their subjects.

If the normal relations between the chiefdoms were friendly, revenge, resulting in killings or uncontrolled fighting, was not in the interest of either landowning clan and the two chiefs with their councils would try to arrive at a settlement by payment of negotiated compensation. But even when public opinion was opposed to

---

[1] Compensation for homicide is now paid in cattle according to a system adopted by the administration and based on Dinka custom. The killer is also subject to penal sanctions.

vengeance being taken, the victim's close kin might wait for an opportunity to kill. Such opportunities sometimes occurred at mortuary ceremonies, when people gathered from many places to drink and dance, and during visits to relatives away from the homeland.[1]

Individual acts of vengeance did not necessarily involve whole populations. The different lineages of a clan have different 'enemies' because of the varied happenings of daily life, in the same way that they have different marriage ties. Whether revenge was taken by the close kin of the victim or by a wider social group depended upon the status of the dead. The death of a chief or of one of his close relatives had a much more disruptive effect than that of, say, a non-landowner attached to a small line. Even so the killings of clients were compensated in order to satisfy powerful and dangerous patrons.

Vengeance parties of landowners were augmented by people linked to them by neighbourhood and political ties. A poor person might or might not get backing from a chief, according as to whether the latter considered a vengeance expedition politically expedient.

Between chiefdoms the main causes of aggression were homicide and the violation of rights in women. Killings resulted from cattle raiding, unsettled wrongs, and the longing to revenge old injuries becoming stronger than other considerations. Offences against women followed upon courtship and marriage across the boundaries of chiefdoms. Minor disputes resulting from theft, insult, and damage to property often remained unsettled because of the distance between the parties concerned and the absence of any judicial mechanisms. They were not regarded as worth fighting about and, unless the people concerned were related in some way, there was no need to maintain good relations. People, then as now, looked upon such annoyances as part of daily life and watched carefully over their property and their behaviour when visiting far afield.

[1] The Mandari also say that a son or a relative of a dead man could watch for an opportunity for vengeance and shoot the killer with an arrow from some convenient cover. He would shout out his name and the name of the person he was avenging and then run off. Revenge was usually taken at night when people were resting round homestead fires unarmed and unprepared and darkness made escape easy. Such action was often regarded as a legitimate way of settling a score and did not lead to vendetta. After three generations the families would come together over a cleansing rite at which a goat was sacrificed and its intestines eaten jointly by both groups, then social intercourse could be resumed.

Divorce cases and those of bride-wealth adjustment between people from different chiefdoms were settled by both parties, in those circumstances where there was mutual interest in continuing to preserve good relations and in the interests of any offspring of the marriage. These were also the kind of cases which might bring together two chiefs and their separate councils.

Small chiefdoms with common frontiers who exploited the same grazing and water and regularly intermarried, say they used arbitration and the payment of compensation. To settle a homicide, a sister or a daughter of the killer or a kinsman of his was placed with the victim's family, who, on the girl's marriage to a third and unrelated party, took the bride-wealth. Cattle were also sometimes paid between people of friendly chiefdoms to compensate homicide, but payments were very high because they were to 'stay the spear', when violence had to be avoided as well as a life replaced. Negotiated compensation was always based on the threat of force except where the parties concerned were kinsmen. A weak chiefdom had no means of compelling peaceful settlement or even of suggesting arbitration should it be against the interests of a stronger party. For negotiations to be effective both sides had to be roughly equivalent in strength and mutually interested. It was the need for negotiating strength that made the Mandari strive to build up the big groups on which they lay so much emphasis.

The fact that hostile relations between chiefdoms could exist over a number of generations in such a small country without mutual interests being completely disrupted is due, I think, to several factors which the Mandari themselves consider to have been important. Chiefdoms were smaller formerly; they were isolated from one another by tracts of bush; there were fewer cattle, and what there were, were largely in the hands of landowners, who planned their movements in accordance with the territorial disposition of affinal kin and political pacts of 'friendship'. Where pastures had to be shared, groups of neighbouring chiefdoms entered into semi-permanent friendly relations with one another, and, therefore, tried to settle disputes amicably. Those others who could afford hostile relations because of the territorial distance between them could indulge in cattle-raiding and acts of retaliation.

Because chiefdoms were localized, fighting could be kept within local bounds. Weaker chiefdoms facing more powerful ones either broke up or redressed the balance of force by allying themselves with a neighbour. There were always chiefs who welcomed an increase in the number of their supporters.

The Mandari say that phrases such as 'we fight so-and-so' do not mean that all the members of a chiefdom regarded all those of the opposing chiefdom as enemies. 'Enemies are one or two.' The hostilities that existed between Jokari and Dari, or Mokido and Dari, were not such that they could not live near one another nor intermarry, although at times relations between them have been very strained. They do, however, imply that their members attend one anothers' ceremonies fully armed and behave with circumspection. Hosts seat visitors with consideration for traditional enmities and enemies are carefully separated by friends: at a mortuary ceremony that I attended near Tali, the Mokido representatives were seated apart from those of Dari because of recent disturbances over the singing of satirical songs. An enemy (*merok*) situation exists between certain Mokido and Dari lines, but nevertheless the son of the recently deceased Dari chief is married to the sister of the chief of Mokido, and during my visit the son of this chief's brother, who has succeeded him, married the daughter of the head of Loriŋa lineage of Mokido. Many people of both chiefdoms have no quarrel with each other, nor have they any relationship to the lineages between whom hostility exists.

Lastly, marriage ties are always stabilizing factors, as people are loth to attack respected in-laws in other chiefdoms on behalf of possibly unrelated neighbours. The killing of an affinal relative of a landowning lineage by a member of a collateral lineage of the same clan could lead to a quarrel between the two lines. Formerly, when mobility was limited by potential or actual hostilities, kinship ties through males and females (*toyuŋi*) gave protection. Youths courted where such ties already existed, going to distant places and staying with maternal relatives for two or three days to meet unrelated girls.[1] Blood relationship, or relationship through marriage, meant safe transit through other peoples' country, as everyone tried to protect the visiting kin of neighbours.

However, one has the impression that a very unsettled and in some ways violent state of affairs existed in pre-administration days. Weak clans are spoken of as having been 'driven away into

---

[1] Eating and drinking with the family of potentially marriageable girls is avoided because eating together denotes kinship and this would make the future marriage incestuous.

the bush', and large ones as having held their position by strength. Undoubtedly the present increase in the population is largely due to the peaceful conditions imposed by the administration. It was, however, always necessary for people to be able to move beyond their chiefdom, and such comings and goings were made possible through an individual's diverse kinship relations. On many occasions people have to meet their in-laws and maternal relatives, who are often not of their own chiefdom. Thus a ceremony, *laka na komayit*, integrates a man into his wife's natal group, making it possible for him to eat and bathe in the homestead of his mother-in-law. Marriage-cattle are exchanged long after marriage; while ceremonies and rites necessary for the health of wives and children are often performed in a wife's natal homestead. A poor suitor who cannot raise sufficient cattle for bride-wealth may supplement by cultivating for his father-in-law. Young people regularly visit mothers' brothers, particularly to collect shea fruit. Mortuary rites, both those of the sweeping of the grave and of the raising of the grave poles, are attended by agnatic and cognatic kin. Apart from these social occasions, visiting relatives of all kinds is a popular pastime, and the kinship interlinking on which it is based has always given safe transit.

Apart from this, Mandari chiefdoms were either too close to each other territorially to permit repeated acts of violence disruptive to mutual interests, or they were too far away for anything like regulated feuding to be carried on. The Mandari lineage and clan structure also did not lend itself to institutionalized feuding. Individual acts of violence did, and still may, take place in response to killings, and, formerly, fighting on a wider scale could bring about complete severance of social relations between enemy lineages living in different countries. Cattle-raiding, both as an act of vengeance and as a means of gaining prestige and property, was also formerly common, big raids being initiated by chiefs. Minor raids also took place until very recently along the Aliab border, where the Dinka impound Mandari cattle moving on to dry-season pastures.[1]

The Mandari like to describe former vengeance and cattle-raiding

[1] During my 1950/2 visit, repeated trouble with Dinka was causing the Mandari to discuss among themselves the possibility of taking all their cattle to Tsera and Köböra grazing instead of to Aliab. Combined meetings of chiefs to discuss problems affecting both the Dinka and the Mandari have now largely resolved grazing problems.

forays. A chiefdom was alerted by drumming from a tree or look-out platform, a signal which was relayed to its boundaries so that all able-bodied adult males could assemble. A sacrifice at which a goat or a chicken was slaughtered was performed at the meeting-tree and the blood was sprinkled on the heaped-up weapons, the following prayer being offered up: 'You God, and you O our Fathers, so-and-so has come and killed our person, now we are preparing to revenge his blood. You arrows fly well, fly well and straight, and do not fall to the ground, fly straight. You our grandfathers help us now, &c.' Each fighter then seized his weapon and went off without looking back and on nearing the enemy hid until just before first light.

Lineages fought together with their affiliated clients, and members of their constituent cattle-fires stood together. The still active older men fought on the outside to keep the fighters together, while the young, inexperienced, and unmarried with no sons to bear their name, were placed on the inside. Tactics were decided by the close agnates of the chief, his personal client and picked fighters, who also kept contact with lineages on the flanks and acted as liaison.

Fighters were spaced to allow room for dodging spears and when a man was killed another took his place. If the fighting was near home the women and boys followed to pick up spears and arrows and assist the wounded. The chief, if able-bodied, fought with his men, and many were killed in this way. Each chief tried to kill his opposite number. Honour was as important as loot and revenge. Men of equal rank on both sides sought each other out while their respective clients tried to protect them by encircling them. If a chief sees an enemy client in front of him he shouts at him to step aside. A client is like vermin ('a wild cat of the bush'); there is no honour in killing him; 'chief killed chief and client killed client.'

After the battle the fighters assembled at the meeting-tree with the looted cattle, and the chief slaughtered a bull or a goat in order to cleanse and protect those who had taken life. The shedding of human blood even when socially justified is a sin which demands purification if sickness is not to result from it. Looted cattle were divided between the lineage heads who took part in the fighting, for their own followers, and child hostages were taken into their captors' families.

When a village was the object of attack, drums were beaten to warn outlying lineages. Women barricaded themselves in their huts while the youths drove the cattle off to the bush.

Alliances are said to have been made for the defence of Mandari country against neighbouring peoples. Mandari Bora, Rume, and Boreŋ chiefdoms say that they combined to repulse the Moru. Dari, Mokido, Bunja, Lorogak, and small chiefdoms near Tali fought the Aliab, two or more chiefdoms sometimes taking part in a defensive action, but each fighting as a separate unit.

One alliance made against the Aliab was as follows. Originally Lorogak owned all the land north of Tali to near the Atuot boundary; this was before Mokido became numerous or Dari had occupied Roro grassland and the surrounding country. Two Dinka groups, Aŋyoon and Korabek, made a friendship pact with Lorogak with a view to occupation of the country of Koto and Beniye within the Mandari border. After a time they became aggressive and tried to push farther south towards Tali river. The chief of Lorogak enlisted the help of the head of the newly arrived Mokido in checking their advance. Some time later these Dinka had an affray with Dari, who, by then, had settled near Roro. Mar Aloŋ of Dakotiaŋ (then chief of Dari) stole some cattle from Aŋyoon who made that an excuse for killing Mar Aloŋ and his eldest son. Mar Desa, then living in Rokwe, mobilized the rest of Dari to fight against the Dinka, and with the help of Lorogak eventually drove them beyond the border. Dari then divided up the land taking one side, while Lorogak and Mokido took the other. A small Dinka group still live in Koto under the chief of Dari and speak Mandari.

The Mandari never had age-sets which could have been linked to a fighting organization. Youths were not initiated and social divisions were based simply on age and sex. In this respect the Mandari differ from the riverain Tsera and Köbora who have a cycle of twelve age-sets of limited social significance but formerly having some bearing on the distribution of fighting strength. During this century, however, Mandari youths have adopted the Atuot initiation ceremonies, known as *Pita na achatni*. These are followed by two months' seclusion, after which the youths enter a 'bead' set known as *Rem* followed by the name of the bead they are wearing at the time after which the set is named. Thus *'Remeyor'* are 'those wearing *Eyor*', a purplish pink bead.

The adoption of bead sets has helped the Mandari to fit into the

Aliab and Atuot cattle-camps where all the male youth is similarly stratified. Beads are worn for the five to ten years when the young people are flirting and courting. But after marriage little interest is taken in them. The middle-aged and old men alive today were neither initiated nor members of bead sets.

III. *The Operation of Force within a Chiefdom*

Within a single chiefdom fighting is inhibited because people are 'brothers'. A large number of the population are, in fact, agnates and the rest will be either clients or old settlers, or affinal or cognatic relatives. People without kinship ties of any kind will be conscious of the feeling of 'brotherhood' that results from common residence and the experiences of everyday life. Killing or shedding blood within a group of 'brothers' in this comprehensive sense is considered socially and morally wrong, although it may happen accidentally or even by intent. The most important function of a chief was the preservation of peace within the chiefdom, and the Mandari say that by and large a good chief succeeded in maintaining this. 'He talked (arbitrated), and that is why we put him there.'

Should talking (arbitration) fail, the chief could, if he were supported by the tree council, threaten to use force to stop two parties fighting. He could muster his own close and collateral kin, and his clients and other people who were loyal to him by virtue of their dependent social position. The chief should always be able to mobilize more executive power than any other group within the chiefdom, but the Mandari say that this did not prevent people sometimes taking private revenge when 'the chief was out of the way'. If fighting broke out in a village, neighbours would try to intervene to prevent bloodshed, since small residential units could not afford to risk the complete disruption that might follow. But even now the irritations of daily life may give rise to situations in which fighting would have resulted if administrative mechanisms were not there to prevent it.[1]

---

[1] A case in point occurred in Dari. A man asked me to treat a stab wound that was bleeding profusely. He said that he had been driving his cattle through the village on the way to Tali when some of them broke loose and trampled on the field of growing seedlings which belonged to a young man of a lineage originally attached to Mar Are of Dari. In the ensuing argument the owner of the field lost his temper, seized a spear with which, as he said, to threaten the herdsman, and

Compensation is never paid for the death of a close agnate, that is, a member of one lineage. Such killing separates the families concerned, 'when kin have shed blood to stay together is unthinkable'; one of the parties goes to live elsewhere after a purification rite has been performed. Cattle can very occasionally be paid for a death between widely separated landowning lineages of a single clan living in different parts of a chiefdom, and no longer receiving the ox of lineage 'brothers' on the marriage of each other's daughters. Such compensation is, however, very rare, and was never paid in females. Usually, members of a single clan (the exogamous group) do not compensate each other. If people are too closely related for cattle to be paid, but they feel some gesture is required of them, they can give animals to the victim's mother's brother, who is within his rights to demand compensation for the death of his sister's son. The mother's brother can also receive compensation for adultery if the adulterer is a member of the husband's lineage.

People of unrelated lines living in one chiefdom pay each other compensation. When this was paid in cattle Mandari say the number of animals was less than those paid for the killing of someone of another chiefdom, since in the latter case fighting might result from the unsettled dispute. Within a chiefdom complete restitution was never possible because the dead man's kin were prevented from taking revenge in the interests of the whole community. If cattle were passed they were regarded as ameliorating the situation only. A purification rite at which both parties ate the entrails of a slaughtered ox, thereby signifying the cessation of vengeful relations, also took place. If people continued to feel bitter the only course of action open to them was to go elsewhere.

IV. *Social Control and Present-day Legal Mechanisms*

There are now two kinds of legal system operating in Mandari. One is based on the pre-administration method of settling disputes

by mistake wounded him. Both parties had been at fault, the herdsman had been negligent at a time when, owing to failure of rain, the people were reduced to near famine, and the destruction of the seedlings could mean starvation for the owner and his family. Serious provocation therefore existed. But a very grave view was taken of the use of a lethal weapon against a neighbour. If people must fight they must do so with the heavy mahogany staves that they carry for protection against dogs and small wild animals. Spears, symbolic of war and raiding, should never be used within the community.

at the individual meeting-trees—now reconstituted as chiefs' 'A' courts which give decisions along the lines of customary law, but are backed by new and wider powers of enforcement. To these have been added the new combined chiefs' courts—the 'B' courts, which are convened quarterly and are attended by the six administrative chiefs. The other system is that operated by the Sudan penal code. The latter is still relatively unimportant as far as the Mandari are concerned, living as they do far from urban centres, but it comes into play in serious cases such as homicide, and when acts are committed against government ordinances or representatives which cannot be finally settled by tribal chiefs.

The 'A' courts (the re-constituted meeting-tree courts), operate over larger political divisions than did the meeting-tree councils of former times, as each is linked up with an administrative chiefdom. Moreover people of formerly dependent status will bring cases before them who would not have brought them previously. Those old councils which have not received recognition still meet as 'unofficial' courts under their own trees and are presided over by the descendants of former chiefs. They talk over minor disputes, passing on those that are unresolved or that demand sentences that only come within the competence of the 'A' courts. Most of the former *toketon* thus function as courts of first instance, though unofficially, while those under the six administrative chiefs have acquired official status and have increased powers.

The meeting-tree courts of former times were spontaneous assemblies with limited powers of enforcement whereas the new 'A' courts are statutorily constituted. The Mandari say that their existence has led to increased litigation, since it has become the thing to do, to litigate. Small disputes, even those between kinsmen, may now come before them. Formerly, minor breaches of custom resulted in ridicule, loss of prestige, or a rough-house, and would not have been brought to the chief for fear of the plaintiff appearing unneighbourly or being accused of acting in a frivolous way. The Mandari express disapproval of the present amount of litigation though they continue to indulge in it.

The old tree-councils met a number of different needs, the satisfaction of pride, and the re-establishment of friendly relations as well as the enforcement of material restitution. These elements are still represented in the 'A' courts, where traditional procedures are retained to a considerable extent. Lineage heads and chief's

personal advisers, including senior retainers, attend 'A' courts even
when they are not, as many are, administrative office holders.
More of the people now taking an active part in judging cases are
probably younger than they were in the old councils, as the administration feels that young office-holders are more easily able to
carry out the administrative duties of the larger chiefdoms than
elders—for example, collecting taxes and volunteers for work on
the roads. The young are also felt to be more 'progressive'. It is
still, however, the elders who largely sway public opinion at court
cases even when they hold no office. Many of the younger office-
holders are sons of former hereditary leaders, while others are from
large client and outsider lines who retain similar positions in the
administrative chiefdoms to those they had in the autonomous
ones. The status of these non-landowning lineage representatives
has become stabilized now that it is official: at the same time it is
derived from the traditional position of their lines in the chiefdom.

Court sessions, which are crowded with ordinary people and
remain informal, are held under the tree of the chiefdom which has
administrative recognition through its chief. The Mandari still
refer to courts as *toket*, not as *lokiko*, a widely used word in the
Southern Sudan and Uganda for the higher 'B' court, a fact which
suggests that they do not consider them to have greatly changed
their function.

The meeting-tree 'A' courts are only brought into being as cases
are brought before them for decision, and their meetings are
arranged to fit in with other social and economic activities. There
is less litigation in the dry season because people are away, though
if urgent cases arise about which strong feelings are aroused, such
as woundings or offences against women, the council is summoned
so that a breach of the peace can be avoided. When a court is sitting
people take the opportunity of bringing minor disputes before it,
but it only meets when there is a demand for justice on the part of
an aggrieved individual. As people with minor problems will come
to the tree at any time when the chief and some elders are there, it
is difficult to draw a distinction between this sort of informal settling of small disputes by a chief with a few elders and the often
prolonged hearing, lasting sometimes for weeks, of a court. People
still come directly to the chief. This is called 'going before the face
of the *Mar*', or 'taking up a stand'. The plaintiff takes up a position
in front of the chief in an attitude that indicates a wish to lodge

a complaint, or sits down obliquely facing him and waits to be questioned. Two litigants may come together, or the accused may be sent for to answer the charge. Formerly he was brought in by the chief's retainers, and the only alternative to presenting himself would have been to flee the country. Resistance to the chief's armed delegation was rarely offered 'because the chief was feared' (respected). Now those failing to attend are fetched by the chief's police.

Written records are not kept of 'A' courts. Both parties to the dispute put their case, then relatives or neighbours give additional information, plead for mercy, or offer personal testimonials. Discursive rhetoric is part of the technique of presenting cases. The members of the council question both plaintiff and defendant and try to assess the real situation. The chief listens during the preliminary inquiries, and when the elders have discoursed and he has decided between the conflicting viewpoints and heard the comments of all members of the court, he sums up, and presents the verdict which has been gradually arrived at throughout the proceedings. Strongly expressed minority opinion among members of the court can protract a case. Formerly, appeal against the chief's summing up, which expressed the views of the council, was difficult, and if a man felt his case had not been satisfactorily dealt with and could not get a change of verdict from the council he had no choice but to move away. Now a right of appeal lies to 'B' court.

A chief's decision was, in general, accepted because 'he is our father', and 'he has his power from God'. He was also made a chief expressly to settle disputes by reason.

There was no sure traditional machinery for settling disputes between individuals belonging to different chiefdoms, although, as I have described, two meeting-tree councils might occasionally combine to settle disputes if both shared important interests. The two chiefs and their councils met on neutral ground, each party grouped under a convenient tree within sight of the other. The chiefs came forward and discussed the case at a central point between them, each was attended by an elder, who reported the proceedings back to the representative councils and brought the councils' opinions back again to the chiefs. This slow and cumbersome method of negotiating through intermediaries was purposely adopted in order to avoid heated argument and fighting. It was used by smaller, closely sited chiefdoms and by adjacent Bora ones.

A Bora elder also told me that the central Mandari Bora *toket* near Tindalu was in early times an assembly to which anyone could bring a difficult case regardless of whether or not he was of Bora stock. My informant considered that its influence as a place where judgements could be obtained was due to the fact that the Bora founder 'came from The Above'. Bora chiefdoms also used this assembly as well as their own councils if they wished.

Peaceful relations between chiefdoms were not, however, mainly dependent on inter-chiefdom machinery of negotiation, but rather on the need to share vital grazing and the restraining presence of dispersed kindred.

Former spontaneous attempts to settle inter-chiefdom disputes have now been formalized by the creation of the 'B' courts. These meet four times a year at Tali in a central courthouse, court records are kept, and they are attended by the six administrative chiefs with their sub-chiefs and headmen and other prominent figures who come to listen. These courts hear major cases and those on appeal. Serious cases from them can be referred to the Province Court at Juba.

v. *The Chief in Traditional Litigation*

A chief was always subject to litigation, though it is said that people were afraid to bring frivolous cases against one, because they 'could endanger their lives by taking away his good name'. Although in theory it is claimed that anyone could complain against him before the elders, in practice a client would not do so.

If a serious case involved an installed chief, a protective and cleansing ritual was performed at its termination to counteract the effect of the angry words and public discussions, which could endanger the chief's spiritual potency. After particularly contentious cases the *toket*, both the council and the tree, were cleansed. A sheep was slaughtered, the meat was eaten by the elders, water was sprayed on them and then poured on the ground at the base of the tree.

A chief sometimes received gifts of animals from rich litigants on the settlement of a long and complicated case. If the giver was related to him the animal was handed to the chief's personal client; if not, it was added to his own herd.

VI. *Extra-legal Mechanisms as a Means of Determining Guilt*

When there was doubt about a case and an accused person continued to protest his innocence, or when witchcraft accusations had been made, oaths were taken and ordeals given by the meeting-tree in order that the truth could be established by supernatural means.

The most common method, which is still used today, was that of 'licking the spear' (*gor memelo*), at which the accused licked the blade of a spear while affirming his innocence. If after a recognized period he had not fallen ill his case was proven.[1]

The meeting-tree also administered ordeals in cases of witchcraft and the evil eye.

VII. *Public Delicts*

While most of the disputes that were settled at the old meeting-trees came under the category of torts, two types of offence came close to being public delicts. One was theft, the other witchcraft and its associated offence, the evil eye.

Theft

Different types of theft did, and indeed still do, evoke different responses, some being regarded as more serious than others. For instance, cattle-raiding between chiefdoms was a legitimate activity as distinct from stealing cattle from someone in one's own chiefdom, which was reprehensible and rarely attempted as it is not possible to conceal the stolen animals. Helping oneself to food or possessions of a chief or a patron with the intention of paying them back at some future time was also allowable.

Seizing property because you consider that it is yours by right was, and still is, not always considered theft, and much animal-stealing falls into this category as legitimate claims may not be met for many years, sometimes indeed a generation may elapse before they are settled. Likewise animals are 'borrowed' on the understanding that they will be returned or a substitute provided.[2]

---

[1] 'The spear cuts the intestines', '*duŋu moynettes*', is supposed to cause symptoms of severe dysentery and other internal disorders which can prove fatal if the swearer is lying.

[2] A representative case occurred in Dari. A man sent a display ox to be tethered in Aliab round the fire of a friend. The latter's son fell ill and an Aliab doctor recommended immediate sacrifice. The sick youth's father had no ox, only fertile cows and a breeding bull, and he therefore sacrificed his friend's display ox. When the friend visited the camp he was promised a female calf

Stealing food can be a very serious offence though a man stealing food for his hungry children in times of plenty will be treated leniently if he makes good the debt. This was especially the case if it was a first offence and the man had a good reputation. When stealing food was motivated by personal greed and became a habit the thief would not only have to make restitution, but might also be taken to the chief's homestead where he would be made to eat great quantities of food in public, which made him both physically ill and the object of ridicule. Food-stealing during famine could lead to a man being beaten up or speared if discovered in the act. Persistent pilferers were also taken before the meeting-tree, where severe fines and sometimes beatings were imposed. The Mandari say the throats of incorrigible thieves were sometimes cut. Those who endangered the lives of others by stealing vital food supplies in times of shortage might also be killed secretly.

The abhorrence Mandari have always felt for the persistent thief bears little relation to the value of the articles stolen (except perhaps for food in time of famine). It is the secrecy of his actions which prevents both his identification and that of his next victim that arouses hatred and fear. It may be this aspect of theft which leads it to be regarded as akin to night-witchcraft. (The night-witch prowls around under cover of darkness trying to take something belonging to his intended victim which he can desecrate and thereby make him sick or die.) Thieves and witches are often equated, and thieves, like witches, being usually poor are likely to be members of weak lines on the fringe of a powerful group. This fact would seem to explain the linking of clients, thieves, and witches in Mandari thought.

Whereas other actions such as fornication and adultery lead to tiresome litigation they do not necessarily lead to social disgrace; but theft is always stigmatized. Like witchcraft, it destroys character; people will not marry into 'thief' lines and girls will not receive notorious thieves in their courting-huts. Thieves will be pointed out, secretly, to the observer and people say 'thieves are evil: they are like witches'.

when a pregnant cow calved. But the cow produced a bull calf. Then an outbreak of cattle-plague killed off most of the friend's cattle, including a newly born female calf and its mother, and the man was totally unable to meet his obligations. After the claimant had made representations to the court it ruled that when, at a future date, the defaulter obtained a female calf either from a bride-wealth payment or from his remaining progeny, it was to be paid over.

In some cases theft can have super-sensory consequences, and the theft of cutting objects, such as spears, knives, and axes, may harm the thief. His 'throat or bowels may be cut' by a following illness with symptoms of knife-like pains in parts of the body. When an axe was stolen from my homestead while I was visiting the Nile, elders who suspected a certain person made him give it up by terrifying him with the probable consequences of his action.

VIII. *Witchcraft*

Every chiefdom is believed to have its witches and persons with the evil eye in the same way as it has landowners, clients, and in-law groups. They are a recognized part of social life. But only when they were thought to have caused deaths or persistent illness was action taken against them.[1] A witch could be expelled in the old days, or finding life intolerable because of the suspicion that surrounded him, he would leave of his own accord if he had relatives elsewhere who would receive him, or he might seek a patron in a distant part of Mandari.

Witches were occasionally killed by members of a friendly chiefdom under cover of a raid, during which the family of the witch would be wiped out and their property seized by the attackers. It was understood that no action would be taken against the raiders who had taken the 'blood' outside the community.

People caught performing acts of witchcraft could be taken before the *toket* and warned, and if they persisted in them and agreement was unanimous, the Mandari say they were executed. Tests were administered to support accusations of guilt carried out either by the chief's own diviner or by taking an oath on a spear. There was a further test (*mönini luga a kulu*) given to witches, at which the suspect was made to drink an infusion of pounded seeds of a certain tree. The innocent vomited immediately and the guilty died after swelling up all over.[2] Witches killed in the waste land and those who died as a result of this test were left unburied. The waste land is the place for defecation; it is where evil and sin are symbolically assigned at rituals and where the bodies of social outcasts were thrown.

---

[1] Now accusations of witchcraft cannot be brought before administrative courts. The only cases are those where medicines are found on the accused, or attempts have been made to use objective poisons; the latter are very rare.

[2] This test is also reported from the Bari.

IX

SOCIAL CONTROL IN CATTLE CAMPS

HITHERTO I have considered the political relations within and between chiefdoms which are territorial units. I now describe the relations between the groups of herdsmen which move backwards and forwards across political boundaries. The Mandari say that when cattle were largely concentrated in the hands of chiefs and members of their landowning lines, movement was more restricted, but there was still the division of economic life, so evident today, into the mobile pastoral activities and the static cultivation of the village fields.

Village life is centred around the growing family, the married and the old; cattle-camp life is focused largely on youth. Many young people, with a sprinkling of older men, live away from home for months at a time, beyond the direct influence of their elders and equally remote from administrative control. Cattle-camp groups have their own regulatory systems suited to their dynamic needs, and a cross-section of young men from different chiefdoms co-operate to obtain the best conditions for all the cattle on the larger dry-season grasslands.

1. *Camp Authority*

Elders do not usually stay long in the camps, as youths and young men do all the herding with the help of their sisters. But if camps are near home older married men and women will spend time in them idling and drinking milk. In camps, authority rests with a son or a younger brother of the chief or his close agnate, who is known as the 'chief of the camp' (*Mar lo Lisuk*), or the 'influential person in the camp' (*ŋutu duŋ lo lisuk*). This is a purely descriptive way of referring to the camp leader and would be used to direct an outsider to him; camp leadership is, therefore, quite different from territorial chiefship, which is an hereditary office for which a man is selected and prepared. The camp leader is simply someone in charge of the chief's cattle, which means that the number of fires under his authority exceeds that of other herders.

He is knowledgeable about cattle husbandry and is an effective organizer; he should command respect and be able to preserve peace in the camp. Camp life undoubtedly has its fascinations and there have been instances of chiefs elect having had their claims to chiefly office invalidated because of having spent all their time in camps instead of being present at the meeting-tree. In the past the roles of political leader, and leader of the cattle, were shared within the chiefly family so that the two types of function should not conflict. This division is also followed today.

The camp leader investigates and settles any disputes that arise, and if he cannot resolve them refers them back to the meeting-tree when the camp draws pegs. In the meantime the disputants are under an obligation to keep the peace. If someone is wounded the leader performs a sacrifice for which the offender gives an ox. This is slaughtered and eaten by both parties to the dispute, the horns being tied to the top of a pole in the centre of the camp as a safeguard against the sickness of humans and animals that might result from bloodshed or quarrelling.[1] The displaying of horns shows that the ceremony of purification has been performed. Mandari say 'God sees the horns and turns aside from punishment and the people remain well.' At the purification ceremony those concerned confess their faults and pledge peaceful intentions.

A killing in a camp is always brought before the meeting-tree, the cattle move to a new site and the camp is abandoned.

When people or cattle fall sick the head of the relevant fire performs a rite with the assistance of the camp leader, but a seriously ill person should be carried to his home so that sacrifice can be offered there under the direction of a diviner and the elders of the family. The camp leader may have to assist at burial if someone dies in a distant camp, one, for instance, in the Aliab.

Every cattle-fire round which the cattle of a lineage or part of a lineage are pegged has its senior young people who are responsible for its discipline and cleanliness. They assist the camp leader in the same way that their fathers assist the chief at the meeting-tree. There is no organization from above, since each member of the camp performs his duties automatically and the leader only

[1] Horns on poles which are the result of sacrifice should not be confused with buffalo horns which people put up when they have killed one.

intervenes at the request of individuals or when the peace of the camp is endangered. Camp life is more elastic than village life because climatic conditions may demand the rapid breaking up and regrouping of a camp. Contact is maintained between camps and villages because people are going backwards and forwards between them even when they are located in the Aliab, and while the day-to-day camp life is in the hands of the herdsmen, the overall movement of the cattle rests with the elders of the meeting-tree. Those on the spot know the state of grass and water and decide which way the cattle should go daily for grazing to ensure an equitable distribution and maximum exploitation of grass, but the movement of the whole herd to a different part of the country or their recall home is decided by the homeland elders after consultation with representative herders.

When disputes arise between members of different chiefdoms encamped on one large grassland the camp leaders meet and try to settle them. Chiefdoms with histories of enmity only use the same grassland if this is unavoidable and if they do so they camp between friendly groups. When camps from different chiefdoms are close together their people attend each other's dances. Their cattle, however, will always graze in different directions. The successful deploying of large numbers of cattle within the limited space available requires great organizing ability.

11. *The Dry Season*[1]

The search for dry-season pastures means movement for all herdsmen except the few who live near good grazing and water and even these move at certain times in order to vary the diet of their cattle. Mijiki lagoon and grazing is used by other chiefdoms as well as by its owners; it is unique in that it has water and surrounding grass sufficient for big concentrations of cattle throughout the dry season. Roro, another lagoon, may be dry by the end of February or March, and the Tapari and Tali rivers almost dry out in some years. In many ways Mandari country is unsuitable for herding, but by careful organization and the use of all available grazing it is possible to keep cattle in reasonably good condition, although they,

---

[1] Reference should be made to the general map at the end of the book which shows the main rivers and grasslands.

like their owners, have to go through periods during which food is barely adequate.

After spending February and March for two years running among the Köbora on the Nile, who have large expanses of open dry-season grazing, plentiful Nile water, and big lagoons surrounded with lush grass and filled with fish and other edible aquatic animals, I was greatly struck by the dry and barren conditions of Mandari country. Shortage of water and grass in Mandari is due to the light, sandy soils and red loams of the ironstone plateau, which do not hold water for long. Depressions that fill up in a shower may be dry by the following day, and inland grass and pools appear only as the wet season with its heavy downpours advances.

For instance, by March all the big pools are dry in Dari, and only a sluggish trickle remains in the river-bed near the villages. All able-bodied people have moved to camps a good distance up the river in open country. Mokido cattle have left their chiefdom and moved down to Mijiki lagoon, and the people who remain behind camp near Tali pool or else walk up to five miles daily to fetch drinking-water. At Mijiki lagoon, I found cattle from Bari Kujutat, Mijiki, Mokido, and other small groups. There were complaints that water was short; Mijiki cattle were using a remaining pool and those of Mokido were drinking from stagnant pools in the dried-up river-beds. Man and animals were existing from day to day awaiting the steady showers that would mean sufficient water nearer home for the cattle, so that they could move back and the people could begin cultivation.

Mandari camps described here are those on the main Mandari grasslands, and those they use on the Nile at Tombek and north of this village in the Aliab. To reach many dry-season camps a long and arduous walk has to be undertaken through rough country where tracks are visible only to the herdsmen.

A dry-season camp is a small replica of a chiefdom. It is named after the landowners who own a large number of the cattle-fires round which the animals are pegged at night. The chief's cattle and those of his kinsmen occupy a central and protected position with the cattle of collateral lineages spread out around them. Scattered on the outside are the cattle of client and settler lines and those of people who are camping with in-laws or mothers' brothers. The central unit tends to keep together throughout the dry season, but visitors and relatives may move to different camps. Grazing conditions sometimes force a camp to divide into two or more parts, but they usually both remain on the same grassland and if they go to a different one they rejoin and go as a single unit.

Cattle leave a chiefdom in a body at the end of the rains, moving forward to intermediate camps near or just outside their chiefdoms as the dry-season grasslands are fired. After a short stay, they move on again to the Aliab, Mijiki, Roro, or Tombek. The following was the constitution of a small intermediate camp of Dari in March on the stretch of Dari river north of Tali; there are camps along this river most years and farther south, at Tali, the same river is used by Jabour, Mokido, and other small clans.

Fires of small Dari camp

Type of lineage	Name of lineage	Number of fires
Landowning	Baŋ lo Are (chief's line)	12
	Dakotiaŋ	4
	Rokwe	4
	Woŋösek	1
	Surukulya	3
Lineages attached	Mandiye	4
through the mother	Baŋ lo Wöröshuk	
	('people' of Mandiye)	1
Client lineages	Korgi (of Rowke)	1
	Nolokoshö ,,	1
	TOTAL	31

Cattle are pegged round fires at night, and a fire-circle may have anything from ten to more than twenty head of cattle, depending on the wealth of the owner and the number of relatives who are tethering their cattle with him. In the Dari camp considered above, the chiefly line had twelve fires—making, with those of the other landowning lineages, a total of twenty-four. The remaining fires were those of the semi-related Mandiye and of two long-standing client lineages attached to Rokwe who peg their cattle separately. The cattle of client families and of individual clients are interspersed with those of their patrons.

There is usually some strategic dispersal of cattle in different camps to insure their owners against loss through cattle-plague and poor condition due to lack of grazing and water, and this makes it impossible to estimate exactly the number of beasts in a man's herd. In the past cattle were so dispersed on account of raiding. Thus, while all the landowning lineages of a chiefdom may be represented in one camp, a camp will not contain all the cattle belonging to the clan and its affiliated peoples.

The Mandari never build permanent camps with cattle byres, and in this they resemble the Aliab Dinka, whose camps are completely mobile. In contrast the Nile-dwelling Tsera and Köbora, who can use the same sites throughout the dry season and whose grazing is accessible to both permanent water and to villages, build palm-thatched dwelling-huts for women and girls in their camps and high, tent-like shelters in the centre of fire-circles for the herdsmen and young animals. In Mandari, girls in camps make use of a shady tree, or a cluster of thorn bushes just beyond the edge of the camp for resting under during the day, and everybody congregates round the fires at night for protection against lion and leopard and herds of buffalo and elephant. Only flimsy roof shelters, a few feet high and without walls, are made for newly born animals, and when it rains people huddle under these. Herdsmen and cattle are outside all the year round, the only permanent animal shelter being the village goat-kraal; this does not accommodate cattle, which rarely enter villages. The Nile groups again differ from the Mandari in having huge village cattle byres.

When cattle from a number of chiefdoms are using one large grassland, herders between whom there are long-standing disputes or recent wrongs try to keep apart, and the Mandari, who know the value of territorial distance as a political factor, exploit spacial separation in relation to the deployment of camps.

If we keep seasonal variability in mind, the chart on p. 141 indicates general dry-season cattle migration and suggests which chiefdoms are likely to be found camping together.

The bracketed groups are those which tend to move together. They are usually composed of people of neighbouring chiefdoms. Combination on this scale is for migration only, and on arrival at the grazing lands the constituent chiefdoms fan out into separately sited camps. When travelling to distant grazing the cattle of one chiefdom move about a hundred yards in front of the following herd, the dust raised by the first herd having barely settled before the observer is enveloped in that raised by the next one. Migrations are always attended by armed herdsmen and are exciting to watch.

The cattle travel slowly to allow girls carrying camp equipment and young children to follow. During the journey the cattle are pegged down in transit camps near water. When the destination is

Clan and its people	Dry season movement Nov./Dec. till Mar./Apr.	Alternative or additional movement	Comments
Jungwa Loci Nyayo and Böndöri Buju Majori Lomore Buntuk Jurkole	(1) Roro (2) Gwir (between Tombek & Boreŋ)	Mijiki	These clans were formerly under the administrative chief of Jungwa. They now form part of Dari administrative chiefship
Dari	Aliab (Pap and Minkerman or Pangmering)	Gwir	Dari exchange grazing regularly with Aliab and marry them
Jabor Jarra	Gwir Sometimes on to Aliab	Mijiki early part of dry season	Parts of all those clans may go to Aliab, lineages which have inter-married with Aliab
Mokido Jokari	as above	as above	
Bari Kujutat and Wombolo	Gwir	Mijiki	
Mijiki	Mijiki	Gwir	
Mandari Bora Boreŋ Rume Gworoŋa	Gwir	(a) Aliab north of Tombek (b) To Tsera at Tombek	Lineages of Mandari Bora often camp at Tombek with Tsera

reached the main body of the herd usually stays for several months or even for the whole of the dry season, although some cattle may be withdrawn from time to time.

During my 1951 visit the Mandari did not use Aliab grazing, or even the boundary grasslands of Khor Gwir, because of a long-drawn-out grazing dispute with the Aliab. They considered the possibility of approaching the Tsera and Köbora for grazing, believing there would be room for all to graze their herds without overcrowding if these were dispersed down the Nile from Tombek to Bolokolite. The Nyangwara already have a dry-season grazing pact of this kind with the Tsera and Köbora, either making their own camps or taking a section of a Köbora one. The Tsera and Köbora in return use Nyangwara woodland wet-season grazing when the Nile floods and their own strip of country is intensively cultivated. Nile island grazing could, no doubt, accommodate more cattle but it is a long way for the cattle of western Mandari to go. They would have to cross their own country and then the waterless belt beyond Tindalu. Such a long trek might debilitate the cattle. Some chiefdoms in the east of Mandari (Rume and Mandari Bora) already use Nile grazing north of Tombek, making an intermediate stop at Khor Gwir. But so far the Mandari have not tried eastward movement on any scale, and I gathered when I revisited them in 1958 that relations with the Aliab were improving.

III. *Wet season*

The cattle movements of the wet season are more varied and individual than those of the dry season. The big concentrations of several chiefdoms on large expanses of grazing break up, and the people of each return separately with their herds to their own forest grazing. There the cattle of landowning lineages graze outside their own villages, making use of wet-season pools and streams, near which the cattle are pegged in a number of small camps or in a single larger one. A grazing place is used for certain months, depending on the work of planting and harvest.

Provided sufficient water has accumulated, woodland grazing outside villages is used in April, so the young men can walk down to cultivate in the early morning. In Dari, cattle occupy camps at from three to ten miles from the main Dari villages. Jabour have camps strung along the banks of Tali river a short distance from their villages. Mokido use other reaches of this river. Jarra and Jokari both have water and woodland. Jungwa, Nyayo, and small clans to the north and west use grassland on the banks of Roro river, while Mijiki stay outside their lagoon. Mandari Bora, having no river, camp near Tindalu where rain-pools form, and Boreŋ and Rume go to Rek.

By June some herds go off again to the Aliab, the River Pap, and beyond, where salt grass—which is necessary for the health of the cattle—grows in abundance. Some of the people return, if not too far away, to help with the August ground-nut harvest.

In September herds may gather for a few weeks at Rek, again for salt grazing. Many return home at the end of October and stay for November while the herders feast on the new harvest and the cattle graze on the stubble. By December the country is beginning to dry out except for places near main rivers and pools. The big grazing lands are fired, and as new grass springs up cattle start dribbling back to them.

Even the small movements of the wet season may, however, be disrupted. Thus in 1952 Mokido could not go to Rek, because of having to cross Boreŋ, with whose people relations were strained, and both Mokido and Boreŋ cattle were suffering from infectious diseases. The Mandari say that it suits cattle to keep moving with only short stops, and that they do so except for the latter months of the dry season. At certain times during the rains they graze as near villages as possible so that the herdsmen can take part in village life. Then women and children have the benefit of milk, and can visit camps to escape from the monotony of the village. Marriages, mortuary ceremonies, and initiations take place and all members of the family are able to participate.

IV. *Atuot and Aliab Camps in Mandari*

Between the completion of planting and weeding and the harvest, Aliab and Atuot herds come to Mandari. They are dotted about the woodland and are owned by people who have a marriage link in the villages near which they camp. Aliab cattle cluster round Tali river where there is a lot of intermarriage between the Aliab and Mokido, Dari and Jabour. The Aliab come in search of a change of grazing for their cattle and some variety in their own diet since they do not cultivate a wide range of crops. In Mandari they find ground-nuts, honey, sesame, and shea-oil. They can be a great liability to their Mandari affinal kin, since they make demands on food when it is at its scarcest.

Forest camps are not used exclusively by any one tribe. When the Aliab or Atuot arrive and find an empty site they peg down; if a camp previously used is occupied they move on. Some camps have been cleared by the Aliab and Atuot, some by the Mandari. Making a camp only involves selecting a good site, near water if possible, clearing trees and undergrowth, and building rough shelters and sleeping frames. All cleared camps are named.

Much is said about the use the Mandari make of Aliab grasslands, and the reciprocal dependence of the Aliab and Atuot on the Mandari for wet-season grass is sometimes ignored. It is true that the Mandari are in greater need of extra grazing, but their co-operation helps to solve Dinka problems also. Economic co-operation between the three tribes will probably increase without any of them losing their particular characteristics or amalgamating on other levels.[1]

Bad feeling sometimes results if Dinka and Mandari herds arrive simultaneously at a Mandari wet-season camp and neither will give way, or if Mandari cultivations are damaged when Dinka herds move through villages at night in order to avoid trekking through the heat. The Mandari say that the Atuot are more amenable than the Aliab, who have a reputation for being bad-mannered and aggressive. They are said, not entirely without reason, to be cattle-thieves. Mandari animals that stray away from main herds are sometimes swept up with returning Aliab cattle, and once over the border they disappear into the vast Aliab hinterland which the Mandari do not like to penetrate.

The Mandari say that in pre-administration days they did not exchange grazing with the Aliab and Atuot but managed fairly well with fewer cattle on their own grasslands. It is difficult to see how they could do so now, with herds at their present strength, and the myths about migration eastwards towards the Nile in search of grassland would seem to indicate that there was always insufficient grazing. All kinds of people who formerly possessed no cattle have acquired small herds.

The Mandari, Aliab, and Atuot are now linked by direct exchanges of grazing as are the Nyangwara with the Köbora and Tsera. The Aliab and Bor Dinka, although they do not exchange

---

[1] There is no exchange of grazing and little intermarriage between Aliab and Tsera and Köbora. The latter have much larger herds than the inland Mandari and do not need to augment them constantly by marrying girls to Dinka. Any marriages that take place are rather between Aliab girls and Köbora men. Köbora and Tsera have ample grazing and their methods of herding cattle resemble those of the Bari and Nyangwara.

grazing with the Tsera and Köbora, have an uneasy relationship with them on account of the pressure on grazing land bordering and opposite Tombek where the Aliab and Bor would like to encroach southwards. Some eastern Mandari also have grazing rights with the Tsera at Tombek.

L

X

INSTITUTIONS REFLECTING POLITICAL RIVALRY

ECONOMIC activities and kinship obligations linking chiefdoms led to much coming and going from one to the other, while political rivalry was created between chiefdoms because of boasted allegiance to individual leaders. Now, rivalry is largely based on the memory of these old loyalties.

Peaceful competition always had a place in inter-chiefdom relationships, as well as hostilities, and was expressed in the chiefly exchanges, honouring dances, competition for the best marriageable girls and for clients, and the efforts made by chiefs to acquire a reputation for lavish entertainment, numbers of cattle, and large bands of retainers.

In the past, to be able to use force to redress wrongs and acquire cattle was, however, the supreme test of superiority. Now the newly introduced initiation ceremonies carried out separately by each chiefdom for its own youths, and the wearing of different kinds of beads by those initiated together, may replace, to some extent, these violent displays of political individualism.

1. *Initiation and 'Bead' Sets*

Initiation, as practised at present in Mandari, originates in its general form from Atuot. Young men speak of having learnt it when visiting Aliab and Atuot cattle-camps and it dates from the economic grazing pacts that were made with Atuot and Aliab in this century. I do not know to what extent initiation rites are identical with those of the Atuot, or whether the Mandari have changed them, or added new elements.

Initiates (*achatni*) undergo a period of testing and trial followed by seclusion, which is again followed by a probationary period after they emerge. This open period varies in length in different places. The important point about the ceremonies is that as soon as the youths of one chiefdom hear that those of a neighbouring one have gone for initiation they hasten to follow suit in order to be eligible to enter the same 'bead set' and wear the corselet-like waist-belt of beads of the colour favoured at that time. No chiefdom wants to be left behind, because this would mean that the young men of other chiefdoms who had already been initiated into the coveted bead set would be courting and securing the favours of the most attractive girls and showing themselves off at dances while its own youth would still be in a more junior bead set or, worse still, uninitiated.

When one group of contemporaries change their beads, as they do at intervals, to those of another colour, those of other chiefdoms change theirs.

The move to go for initiation is made in the first instance by youths who have reached the appropriate age, and it is supported by parents and elders who make the necessary arrangements. Towards the end of the period of seclusion and during the subsequent 'open' weeks or months, initiates tour Mandari country in bands looking for similar groups with whom to fight and for unrelated girls from whom they can collect forfeits. Each band is led by an older man who has an assistant; both are armed in order that they may protect the band should it pass through hostile country. The initiates walk in formation and carry ornamented sticks which they have carved during their seclusion. Their aim is to collect forfeits and be seen and admired. When they meet other bands they fight and wrestle with them so that, should they win, the girls will hear about it and favour them.

People who are initiated together help each other in various ways in later life especially during courtship and early adulthood. Though initiation emphasizes the solidarity of young men of the same age in a chiefdom, such solidarity is not new to the Mandari. It is only the form that it now takes which is new. Moreover, while bands of young men from different chiefdoms may be rivals, friendships may also be formed across political boundaries; the villages of the smaller chiefdoms are so close that they can if they wish synchronize their initiation ceremonies although this does not happen in larger ones. A youth of one chiefdom can make friends among youths of the same bead set of another, and I know of such friendships where the villages of two landowning clans were only separated by a road. This would be less likely where relations between the two chiefdoms were traditionally hostile.

Because Mandari bead sets have developed recently, at a time when the age-set systems of most African peoples are disintegrating, they played no part in the indigenous political organization.

11. *Attacking Songs*

Another way of expressing inter-chiefdom rivalry has always been the composing of songs which are sung by the members of one chiefdom against those of another at dances. Songs strike at many aspects of peoples' lives—suspicion of witchcraft and the evil eye, breaches of customary behaviour—or anything which is a matter of moment, such as the killing of a chief, famine, or fighting. Two songs were even composed for the dance that was held when I left Mandari, one by the young men of Mandiye lineage near whose hamlet I lived and the other by the Dari 'B' court clerk.

Songs are not necessarily composed by, nor do they always belong to, landowners, but once sung at a public occasion they are adopted by the chiefdom to which the composers belong and are thereafter part of its song repertoire, particularly for singing at dancing during mortuary ceremonies. Although it is always known who owns the song and whom it is sung against, other people may dance to it or sing it; but the singers who introduce it at a dance are usually from the owning chiefdom. Some songs arouse very bad feeling in the chiefdom against which they are directed; then the offended persons are unlikely to add to the popularity of the songs by using them.

The administration has now also become a universal target of songs. It came into being backed by powerful alien forces and in many cases drastically altered peoples' lives by the amalgamation of chiefdoms, the recruitment of workers for road-making and other projects, and the setting up of new judicial mechanisms. Songs are directed against it as they are against rival Mandari chiefdoms, and many others make passing references to government activities. Singing against the government must be seen in the whole context of attacking songs. Because it is the object of criticism in song it is not necessarily hated any more than a rival chiefdom is hated. Exasperation, affection, hostility, and respect are all to be found in the attitude the Mandari take towards the administration. Its actions sometimes make people angry or are considered to be unfair. The accidental death of a man doing voluntary government work on the roads will now be the subject of a song in the same way as a man's death from a rival's spear was formerly. Such a death cannot be ignored any more than the actions of traditional rivals could be ignored. Therefore, the government is attacked in the same way as was any group that transgressed a chiefdom's autonomy. When people talk about the administration in other contexts they concede its advantages—the establishment of public security 'which allowed the villages to fill with young people', the help given in times of famine, the integrity of decisions given in the courts, where 'everyone gets his due'.

The three songs given here may seem perhaps to over emphasize the anti-government theme but they are typical of the kind of references that are made to the object of an attack in all clan songs.

Song of Mokido clan

Mandari text	English text
Miri na Tali a naron.	The Tali government is oppressive
Nu parana ku ririŋa na ŋutu	Passing its time in harsh correction
A jaran noga.	Escape is only in the grave!
Adi, Miri na, wunja.	The government dissembles.
Gurak yalari Gareŋ lo Akur,	Gurak is added to Gereŋ lo Akur
A lukata Mariiyal.	And there also Mariiyal and Mabour
Mabour joŋa i togu na mere—	are taken to chop at the mountain
Mar Iyoŋ, twan ŋukon yi a naron.	
Bare turya: logu'di lu joka	Oh Chief Iyoŋ, death has dealt cruelly with us!
A yi luŋa miia—kutuk na Siti na Burun!	Select beaters; beans are there being pounded.
Twan ŋu kon yi anaron!	And we have been called in our multitudes—
Uŋgwö ŋu tulunda	(by) The complaints of Burun's wife.
	Death has defeated us! The foreigners have swept over us!

The translation of Mandari songs presents many difficulties. They are full of brief and often ambiguous references to past and current events, which can only be properly understood if the full context is known. I have tried, with Mandari help, to express as far as possible the feelings the songs embody. It has been necessary to include a short explanatory text for each song.

Analysis of the first song

This song is a lament against what were felt to be the harsh and unreasonable demands of the earlier administration, particularly those for heavy road labour and porterage. It is implied that only the dead are left alone, and that these probably died from overwork. (People particularly stress the load-carrying, when trekking was done on foot, and say some carriers suffered from ruptures.)

'The government dissembles' refers to the 'bribing' with offers of money, which led Mandari to volunteer for work without realizing quite what was entailed. Gereŋ Akur has died during government work, then Gurak dies also. 'Chop at the mountain' means cut stones from one of the ironstone outcrops for road foundations. Chief Iyoŋ is Chief Korondo, former government chief of Dari. The beans that are being pounded are for sale for hut-tax imposed by government. The two lines before the last refer to a complaint made about the condition of the road by the wife of a District Commissioner (a Mr. Brown?). As a result everyone was made to go out and repair it. '*Uŋgwö*' in the Mandari text means 'foreigners'. (Government administrators are also known as '*Miri*', or '*Aseken*' (mainly used for northern Sudanese). '*Akuma*' also means 'government'.)

Song of Nyayo clan

Mandari	English
I	**I**
Gajuk lo Aku ta kökökin grusun ada?	Gajuk lo Aku, how is it you are leaving the money?
Akuma apo a nikaŋ,	The government has arrived and is ours.
Twan ana a nikaŋ ku Dari.	
Nyiyo lo Are lu, i söpö a mini	And this is our 'death' and that of Dari.
Yi topakin i kak na Dupi.	'They make rings round' the son of Are.
	And we have landed up in the country of the Moru.
II	**II**
Gwörö gwugwuju na—	Gwörö (a wild cat) is barking there—
Remeri kayo lo 'Bunit ko Aŋyun	The first-born son of 'Bunit has been pierced with the butt of a spear,
Be yi 'aying kata—	
Maderon a peja ide?	But we were not there!
Yi kikidem mire na karo	You, administrative chiefs, will you not inquire into this?
Aba gwegween nolitan,	
A yi wörö dani? Maderon ta nyala deba?	We are working for the administration of the (dead) first-born

Our father's tears flow
And where shall we now go?
Oh chiefs, will you be willing to
recompense us?

III

Laser likaŋ ŋu remu, Nyiyo lo Aba.
Yi kona se kita na tato
Nonana inyat nikaŋ dedena beron
Wiri likaŋ lowya.
Miri na Tali tin ŋutu yoka dengeli!

III

Our brother has been speared. Oh
child of my Father.
Our labour has become without
interest.
(But) Our arrow-shafts were known
of old
The poison of our arrows!
The government of Tali makes one
spew up bile!

Analysis of the second song—verse I

Reference is made to Gajuk Aku, who joined the Sudan Army, but left because he did not like it. This 'death' is the eclipse of independence and sovereignty under government amalgamations. (Nyayo is now joined to Dari.) 'The son of Are' may be the Dari chief, grandson of Are. 'söpö a mini'—'deceived like a bush-cat', is a Mandari saying similar to 'make rings round someone'. The last line refers to a work party which was sent to Moru country.

Verse II

This verse deals with the death of Bunit's son while his kinsmen were away on government work. He has been stabbed with the sharpened metal butt of a spear. The 'chiefs' challenged in the middle of the verse and in the last line are administrative chiefs and they are asked whether they are willing to recompense the people for their tribulations now they have taken over from the original leaders. (This part is a hit at administrative chiefs.)

Verse III

The key to this verse, which reiterates Bunit's death, is in the last line. It contrasts the boredom of the new régime with the glory of the old days, viz. 'our arrows', &c. Nyayo, the singers, were formerly a famous fighting clan with their own Mar. Dengele is the Mandari word for the gall-bladder of a chicken, hence it is used here to describe the bitterness of the vomit of disgust which is like gall.

Song of Mijiki clan

Mandari	*English*
I	**I**
Nyiyo lo Jabor alo, ŋu yukin i kurusi.	The son of Jabor is idling in the seat of office.
Inglisi, yi a wokakin wörö a kaya ki'yu!	Oh, English, we cannot reach the heights you set us!
Mukök na Inglisi	Oh heritage of the English, and you
A ta Aseken, töyuŋi ku Bari	other strangers who claim
Porda na Mariyaŋe, yi a wokakin!	brotherhood with the Bari.
	We, clan of Mariyaŋe, we can no longer compete.
II	**II**
Ku momor ŋutu a jur liŋ	All of us are now joined as one
A ta ku mandu dija na roba ana?	country,
A gwa sana.	And don't you regret the dying out
Nonana ku Ba, luga a wusut ko gila.	of this, our stronghold?
A ta a mandu kösöröt lo ki alo,	And what it has become?
Madir Mayanne, do alo lalaŋ Mar Lokwe!	Which in the old times under our fathers, was a centre of fame among foreigners.
	You hate even the stars above us.
	But Mayanne, Oh, you excel even the White Chief!

This is a protest song against the amalgamation of the old chiefdom of Mijiki with that of Jabour, and its placing under Jabour administrative chief.

Analysis of the third song—verse I

Line one refers to the Jabour chief who now holds office over Mijiki. The rest of the verse comments on the high administrative standards expected, which are followed by the Bari and more advanced tribes. Mijiki feel it is beyond their powers to attain them.

Verse II

Again there is reference to the merging of Mijiki with Jabour. (Their demise began with the war against the Moru, see p. 53, which destroyed their population. The administration felt they no longer had sufficient numbers to warrant an independent chiefship.) Mijiki recall the time when their country was a famous centre of hospitality known beyond Mandari. '*Mayanne*', in the last line, is Kulaŋ Shuli, last chief of Mijiki. In his time amalgamation took place, and he was appointed a government sub-chief. Mijiki extol him as excelling even the District Commissioner (white chief).

Mandari songs are pervaded by a nostalgia for lost sovereignty. They also reflect another modern political tendency, that of seeing the present chiefly office as divided. The 'Government chief' (*mar lo miri*) is not necessarily the same for them as the 'chief of the homeland' (*mar lo bay*). They recognize government chiefs, but they also recognize the influence and authority of other leading elders when the latter are the descendants of former traditional office-holders. These two kinds of leadership run parallel in many places. Political office over an administrative division may not be filled by a traditional landowning leader, and some units in the administrative combinations will be excluded from independent power and authority. When an old chiefdom has been placed under an office-holder of a larger neighbour, recognition is given to the office-holder on the purely political level. His influence does not necessarily, nor does he try to make it, extend beyond this. The Mandari comment on the change in chiefship, saying, 'In the past important leaders were given by God: now everyone thinks he is *mar*.'

XI

THE POSITION OF THE MANDARI IN THE NILO-HAMITIC/NILOTIC CONTEXT

IT is clear that the Mandari are in no sense a tribe or even a single people; but rather the product of different stocks, some claiming to be indigenous, others the descendants of individuals or groups who found their way into Mandari. Some of these came from the Nilotic north, others from the Bari-speaking south, and beyond. While intermingling is always found on the boundaries of tribes or peoples and is the natural result of coming and going across a marginal area, the Mandari population is mixed over the whole country.

Further, their pivotal position between the Nilotic and the Nilo-Hamitic blocks and the continual impact of these two neighbouring cultures complicates the issue already touched on, as to how Mandari should be classified—if indeed they can be satisfactorily classified at all on the available evidence. It is certain that the Bora element in the population is central to this problem and it is a pity we cannot know for certain who they originally were. Bora people are not unique to Mandari; in fact this name occurs widely in Equatorial Sudan and Uganda. Father Crazzolara, in his analysis of the migrating Luo tribes, refers to 'Bura' and 'Vora' time and again.[1] He finds the name generally crops up in countries overrun by Luo stocks, or among Luo speakers themselves.

Writing of Luo migrations from Wi-puri to Lafon Hill he says the Luo rested at Lafon then departed south to mountains, 'in the region of Lirya, of old called Bura'.[2] Again, referring to Lafon, he recalls the arrival of 'groups of Ademac and Bupi, part of the broader denomination of Bura'.

[1] As regards his spelling of 'Bora', Crazzolara uses a 'u', but says that this resembles the sound 'oo' as in 'poor'. See his study of *The Acooli Language*, International Institute of African Languages and Cultures, Oxford, 1938. When 'Bora' occurs among the Moru, the 'b' becomes 'v'.

[2] Crazzolara, *The Lwoo Migrations*, Instituto Missioni Africane, Verona, 1950, part i, chap. ix.

In Uganda among the Pajok, 'a Luo-blend speaking Acholi or Luo', he finds a Bura clan and country.[1] Among Patiko, Acholi by origin, a 'clan or tribal group of Bura' appears. Bura is here the name of the 'old royal court of the chiefs (*rwoths*)'. A common saying among these people is, 'it is as pleasant as at Bura'—implying that those who left compared places favourably or the reverse with the old Bura country.

Crazzolara claims that the name Bura 'must have been great and famous', and that it had many meanings—it appears as a 'clan group', 'a kinship group', 'a court'. It is sometimes of 'a mythic nature', and in this respect he says it is always connected with 'old Madi-land'. There is often equivalence of Bura with 'royal'—'the residence of the *rwot* was simply called Bura, as if this were the name of the royal clan.' In some Acholi, 'Bura was the place of assembly and the assembly itself'.

In the Sudan, Bura and Vora are names of territorial regions on the Juba–Torit road. Crazzolara suggests that the Bura may have once lived on the Nile near Rejaf, and that a fairly large area to the east from Lirya towards modern Torit, north of the Okari mountains, was inhabited by people calling themselves Bura.

In well-separated tribal areas Crazzolara found Bura. Sometimes he believes them to be the aboriginals—'often they are the most respected', and 'the head of each group is the chief. He is also the rain-maker for the area.'

He concludes that the Bura were a powerful pre-Madi stock who, after the dispersal of the Madi by Luo-speaking peoples, retained their original high social position. He suggests that many moved off with the dispersing Madi and were assimilated and obtained positions of eminence elsewhere.

It seems certain that the Mandari Bora have a connexion with these other Bora. In Mandari, 'Bora' is primarily a place: a cradle-land—'the country of Mandari Bora from which everybody divided out'. Bora people dispersed over Mandari and on to the Nile know of their single origin and speak almost nostalgically of the old Bora homeland. There remains a Mandari Bora clan claiming to be the senior branch of the original nucleus. The high status of Bora lines and their association with rain-powers point up similarities with the 'Bura' of Crazzolara.

It cannot be known whether the Mandari Bora are part of an old

[1] Crazzolara, *The Lwoo*, Verona, 1954, part iii, pp. 336–8.

landowning and formerly much larger group still *in situ*, or are people who came from elsewhere and brought their name and associations with them, or whether an indigenous Bora stock moved off and their land and name were taken over by infiltrators (possibly of Luo stock). One of the last two answers may be the most likely, in view of the dramatic arrival of the Bora ancestor in the Bora myths, and the way in which small mountains in this part of the Sudan feature as stopping places for migrations.

If we compare Mandari chiefship with what Crazzolara says about chiefship in scattered Luo-speaking groups, particularly Acholi, similarities are apparent. In an Acholi group at Aleero in Uganda, Crazzolara speaks of the installation of the chief, which took three days, and at which he was washed and oiled. He sat on a royal stool, and had special beads and drums.

Among the Atyak, an Acholi group who became 'Luoized', a clan leader (*ladit*) (not of the royal clan) was seated at the side of the chief at his installation, and both were washed and anointed with oil and butter.[1] At Patiko (Acholi) 'a kind of interpreter or mediator (*ladom*)' who acted for the chief, 'who did not mix indiscriminately with petitioners', appears. Crazzolara noted that 'foreigners could easily be led to think these *ladom* were important persons', and 'that in more recent times some were actually enticed to betray his sovereign and take his place'.

I have stressed certain similarities between the Mandari and Nilotics of the Acholi/Luo group, because it has generally been assumed the Mandari are merely an offshoot of the Bari. I doubt, however, that the situation is so simple.

This does not mean that I am not aware of their extensive common ground with the Bari, which Mandari themselves also stress. Identity is most obvious, of course, in language. (Although many key Mandari words show Nilotic affinities, one example being the old Mandari greeting *mötö*—now largely replaced by the Aliab *kudwal*—which is like the Acholi *moto*, to greet. Varying forms of this word occur in other Nilotic societies.) From a survey of the material on the Bari it would seem that their territorial and political divisions were very like those of Mandari.[2] There is a Bari office of father-of-the-land (*monyekak*), but it is not quite clear how this

---

[1] Crazzolara, *The Lwoo Migrations*, part ii, chap. xiii.

[2] *The Bari*, an unpublished note prepared by myself from literary sources before my visit to Mandari.

office fitted into the Bari political system. Some *monyekak* are spoken of as 'purely ritual functionaries', others as 'political leaders', some as 'rain-makers'. These statements could be referring to what also happens to Mandari chiefship when the various roles of chiefly office become separated. Father Spagnolo gives a Bari text describing the installation of the father-of-the-land; but it is not really very like the installation of the Mandari *mar*.[1] I think that Mandari chiefship may be the result of the merging of two kinds of office. It could be significant that early non-Bora landowners—Wejur, Lorogak, Böndöri-Nyayo, and others—speak of having 'chiefs' when the Mandari Bora were concentrated at Tindalu under their leader Mar Nykwac and prior to their infiltration of the surrounding country.

Among the Bari social classes are very sharply defined and opposed and there are several of them. The Bari also had simple age sets which are traditional; the Mandari did not. I would suggest that, by and large, Nilo-Hamitic elements are stronger in the Bari and southern Bari tribes, and Nilotic influences more widespread in the Mandari.

[1] Spagnolo, *Bari Grammar*, Missioni Africane, Verona, 1933, p. 322.

APPENDIX

LANDOWNING CLANS AND THEIR ATTACHED LINEAGES

* indicates clans which are now dominant, but whose founders came from outside Mandari.

LANDOWNING CLAN			CLIENT OR OTHER LINEAGE			
Name of landowning clan	Landowning lineage to which outsider attached	Client lineages	Came from	Settler lineage	Came from	Early landowning, or displaced, lineage or clan
*DARI CLAN	ROKWE LINEAGE	1. BARIIYE	'Bot Yu', 'the South' Terekeka?	1. NOLOKOSKO (Sister's sons)		
		2. KORGI	To Chief Apat from Korgi of Terekeka.			
		3. UNNAMED FAMILY	From the bush to Chief Apat. Married sister of ancestor of Bariiye.			
	SURUKULYA LINEAGE	AGARAŊ	From Atuot to Chief Akweir.			
	DAKOTIAŊ LINEAGE	NONE		NONE		
	WOŊÖSEK LINEAGE	UNNAMED FAMILY	Came to Böki, Woŋösek ancestor. Aliab Dinka.			
	DARI (BAŊ LO ARE)	BAŊ LO KULAŊ	ALIAB	YARE	Jokari. Sister's sons of Nolija part of Baŋ lo Are.	
	DARI (BAŊ LO ARE)	'People' of NOLIJA TOKEBA	Jabour, stayed with Yare, sister's sons of Nolija.			

		NYIROM	JABOUR	MANDIYE	From illegitimate son of wife of Mar Are.	
*JABOUR (from KIC DINKA and displaced WEJUR landowners).	KAWÖRI	MALUɲDIT	A single Dinka attached to Chief of Dari (now deceased).			
		JUNGURE	?	PAKURJU	Mandari Bora —two brothers to find fish.	WEJUR: former owners of country / IOM: ,, ,, / BANYEJUR: ,, ,,
		DORE	Clients of Wejur displaced landowners—see last column.			
*MOKIDO (from MORU)	JAMIɲA		Have clients but particulars not available.	JAMIɲA and BUKO	Descended from wives of mother's brother of Chief Desa.	GOLA / JAMBEKE } divided land in old days with LOROGAK / LOROGAK, former owners of the country.
BUNJA	MANDYA	KORONDA	Ancestor stolen from Mandari Bora as a child. Stolen from Rume.			
		JAKARI MANDARI	,, ,, ,,			
JURKOLE	JURKOLE (small clan not segmented)	GUMORO	Aliab to founder of Jurkole, Kopogo.			
		KUNJURO	Buju clan—two brothers fought.			

LANDOWNING CLAN		CLIENT OR OTHER LINEAGE				
Name of landowning clan	Landowning lineage to which outsider attached	Client lineages	Came from	Settler lineage	Came from	Early landowning, or displaced, lineage or clan
JARRA		TIJÖKÖR	Not sure if clients or settlers.			
		JUME (KOKA)	Found in bush spearing leopards (*koka*).			
		REDYA	Originally clients. Now inter-married and live with line of Chief Moke.			
BARI KUJUTAT	BARI TAPAR DAMADAN	NYÖRI	GWOROŊA	MAYA	BORA	GÖLÖRI. Had land in old days.
		FADIER	ALIAB			
JOKARI		PIRIYE	Came with Jokari from Mandari Bora.	METE	BUJU. Divided after a death, came with cattle.	LEKELYU. Owned land— now very few.
		JOKARI-JÖŊÖ	Aliab			POBI. Owned the grazing and swamp.
		Another un-named family	Aliab	DIGDAR	BOREŊ to Chief Kila Jambe of Jokari.	

INDEX